Approaching the Canticle

*St. John of the Cross
for the Marathon Runner*

ANTONIO AGUIRRE VILA-CORO MD, PHD
*Secular Oblate, Benedictine Abbey of
St. Domingo de Silos, Spain*

Approaching the Canticle: St. John of the Cross for the Marathon Runner
by Antonio Aguirre Vila-Coro MD, PhD

Cover Design by Atinad Designs.

© Copyright 2015

SAINT PAUL PRESS, DALLAS, TEXAS

First Printing, 2015

All rights reserved. No part of this publication may be reproduced, stored in a retrieval system, or transmitted in any form or by any means, electronic, mechanical, photocopying, recording, or otherwise, without the prior permission of the copyright owner, except for brief quotations included in a review of the book.

All scripture quotations are taken from various editions of the Catholic Bible, as discussed in the Introduction.

ISBN-10: 0996324127
ISBN-13: 978-0-9963241-2-0

Printed in the U.S.A.

Approaching the Canticle

The ultimate reason to run is love (stanza 38).

To Aco, who runs with silence.

Foreword

In the XXIst Century, in the so-called Developed World many of us spend a large part of our time running around with multiple occupations. Most of us have, nevertheless, the option of pausing for a moment and taking a look at a poem. On another hand, to stay in good shape some of us practice one sport or another, for example, jogging. The person training for a Marathon may be advised to run its 42 km spread over a week's time to gain the fitness needed to run the whole distance in one go on the day of the Marathon run. The amount of time used to that effect is more than enough to read this booklet. It is enough time even to memorize the whole poem in less than one year during the training, at a pace of one stanza per week.

St. John of the Cross composed his poem, *The Spiritual Canticle*, while in prison in Toledo. Later, he added a lengthy commentary in prose, which is one of the most important works of mystic literature of all times. His commentary is full of doctrine, and he makes frequent Bible quotations to provide a theological support for his experiences[1]. When choosing his wording for some of his stanzas and comments, it is quite apparent that he looked at the literal wording of the Bible as he knew it, for example in Stanza 31 (one eye, one hair).

He was reluctant in commenting on his stanzas *not to narrow them down to a meaning unadaptable to every palate.* According to his own words, *these stanzas were composed in a love flowing from abundant mystical understanding. I cannot explain them adequately, nor is my intention to do so…for mystical wisdom, which comes through love…need not to be understood distinctly in order to cause love…we love God without understanding him*[2].

We have, nevertheless, dared to shorten his commentary even further and to edit at our leisure his words and his quotations, in the hope that those who have read his original will forgive our boldness, and those who have not read it will become inspired to read it. We have tried to limit ourselves to transcribe in today's language the symbolic meaning that he personally explained, and to summarize those main ideas of his that refer just to the poem. We have intentionally removed most of his text referring to doctrine in an attempt to keep just the beauty of the poem and its allegorical meaning. Perhaps reading the poem or remembering a stanza may bring the reader to hear the gentle whistle of the Shepherd, to use the words of St. Theresa of Ávila when she talks about the *Prayer of Passive Recollection*[3].

For the Scripture quotations we've used the Jerusalem Bible[4] or a XVIIIth Century Douay English translation from the Vulgate[5]. Occasionally, we have used a Latin edition from the XVIth Century[6], courtesy of the Library of the Benedictine Abbey of Santo Domingo de Silos. Its text is identical to the Latin text accessible to St. John of the Cross, and has allowed us to keep citations as he knew them, for example reference 40.2. At other times we have taken the citation with the literal wording of St. John of the Cross in his original text. We have avoided using the New American Bible Revised Edition, Catholic Edition, whose foreword in some editions mentions a *Current Era* rather than a *Christian Era*; it also enunciates the fifth commandment as *you shall not murder* (instead of *you shall not kill*); it eliminates, perhaps as a concession to members of another religion, the word Yahweh[7-9], and changes Isaiah 7:14. Its translation is no longer *...a virgin will conceive, and bear a son...* Now it is *... a young woman will conceive...* We have not used the New Jerusalem Bible either, which also enunciates the Fifth Commandment as *you shall not murder*, perhaps planting a seed to change 2,000 years of teaching of the Church. For the Psalms, we usually quoted text from the Jerusalem Bible, but we have kept the original Christian numeration from the Vulgate.

When referring to the various components of the human being we have used the following terms:

Soul: the immaterial, immortal component of the person, whose attributes could perhaps be Existence, Awareness, and Bliss[10].

Mind: the remaining of the intangible part of the person, comprising the **intellect**, the **will**, and the mind's **non-conscious** content.

The poem consists of a dialogue between God and the person who moves toward Him by prayer and self-giving. As the poem progresses, the person advances by increasingly giving his love to God. This results in a transformation, whose description we try to facilitate by using the following terms:

Wayfarer: includes all human beings. Initially they walk toward God unknowingly; later, and that is the starting point of the Canticle, some walk with full awareness of what is the object of their search. The Wayfarer advances along stanzas 1-12 through the so-called *Purgative or Ascetic Way*, with impatient longings of love; he uses the knowledge of self, disdaining pleasures and overcoming difficulties (stanzas 1-3); he searches the knowledge of God and asks the irrational creatures (stanzas 4-6), the rational creatures (stanzas 7-8), the Beloved (stanzas 9-11), and finally searches God by faith (stanza 12).

Bride: the Wayfarer is transformed in her when he finds the Beloved in encounters of union of love with *spiritual betrothal*; she walks along the *Contemplative or Illuminative Way*, and she continues working with urgent longings of obtaining full freedom of the inner and outer obstacles that make union difficult. She and the Beloved sing stanzas 13-21.

Spouse: she has united herself to God in *spiritual marriage*. She walks along the *Unitive Way*, in *transforming union*. She has calmed the imaginations and appetites (**foxes**, stanza 16), has stopped the dryness in prayer (**wind of the North**, stanza 17), has calmed her mind (**nymphs of Judea,** stanza 18) and has obtained the breeze of the Holy Spirit (**wind of the South**, stanza 17), which gives her the *spiritual marriage*.

The self-giving of the Spouse in love is now perfect and the union is complete, like the light of a candle with the light of the sun. Spouse and Beloved then sing stanzas 22-40. Stanza 20 summarizes the *Unitive Way*; this is further detailed in stanzas 26-30: gifts received by the Spouse when she gives herself to the Beloved (stanzas 26-27), love as the highest personal achievement (stanza 28) and as the highest form of service to the Church; stanza 30 sings the Beloved and the Spouse working together as one single being. To avoid any possible confusion from the word *spouse* meaning in English either one of the spouses, we have kept **Spouse** to refer only to the human being. God is referred to as **Beloved** or **Bridegroom.**

The final steps of the Wayfarer—Bride—Spouse are sung in stanzas 36-40, where St. John of the Cross tries to explain how a *transformation in God* occurs. The soul is literally transformed in divine; the light of the candle and the light of the sun become permanently united. The soul and the Father are one; this allowed St John of the Cross to draw the Crucified as the Father would see him, looking from above. This perspective of the Crucified is unique in the history of art; the drawing is reproduced in the front cover of this booklet.

The whole Canticle spins around love. In our opinion, St. John of the Cross understands love as the giving of one person to another; an abandonment of herself to donate the whole of her person to the relationship, to the Beloved. This love can be perceived in many different ways. The central theme of the Canticle is its perception as *absence*, already shown in the first verse, **Where did you hide, Beloved, and left me moaning?** In other stanzas this love is perceived as *emptiness, pain, or suffering*, although none of those destroy the lover because she accepts them as coming from the Beloved. For this reason, St. John of the Cross expresses this love in his poem *The living flame of love* with terms such as *delightful wound, sweet cautery, tenderly wounds my soul, in killing you changed death to life…*[11].

On other occasions, this same love is experienced as *gushes of sweetest feelings* like the **touch of a spark, the spiced wine,** in stanza 25. In the absence of love, some of those feelings would be unpleasant, but the presence of love in the Wayfarer causes those same feelings to be most welcomed. It is in this sense that the Blessings of the Sermon of the Mount could be translated as *Congratulations to those who weep…*(Matthew 5:5). Suffering is undoubtedly real and destructive, but the Wayfarer can transform it into a *blessed night* by means of love, i.e., by means of donating his own will to the Beloved, with full and unconditional acceptance of the pain. In such a case the *night* becomes the place of encounter for the lovers[12]: *Oh night that joined Beloved with lover, lover transformed in the Beloved!*

At the top of the page we have entered a poetical English translation of a stanza, followed by the original in Spanish, and a literal translation of the Spanish in **bold** underneath. At the end of the comment we have written a symbolic translation for each stanza.

We thank the Librarian Monk of the Benedictine Abbey of Santo Domingo de Silos for his help, and two Discalced Carmelite Cloistered nuns, one from the Convent of the Encarnación in Ávila and one from the Monastery of the Most Holy Trinity, St. Charles Square, London, for their comments to the manuscript.

A. Aguirre Vila-Coro
aaguirrevc@gmail.com

1.
Search of the Beloved

- Purgative way of the beginners

- First steps on the spiritual journey

- The knowledge of one's self starts (*)

- Longings of impatient love

(*) The knowledge of oneself is the starting point, the path, and the goal.

Symbolic translation:

My God, where do You hide within me? After a fleeting glimpse of Your love, I painfully long for the manifest presence of Your divine essence and for my perception of Your love; I thus abandon everything to seek You alone.

2

Oh shepherds, you that yonder,
Go through the sheepfolds of the slope on high.
If you, as there you wander,
Should chance my love to spy,
Tell him that I suffer, grieve, and die.

Pastores los que fuerdes
allá por las majadas al otero,
si por ventura vierdes
aquel que yo mas quiero,
decidle que adolezco, peno y muero.

Shepherds, those of you who go up through the sheepfolds to the hill, if by chance you see Him I love most, tell Him I am sick, I suffer, and I die.[1]

Shepherds are the intercessors (desires, affections, moanings). God communicates something of Himself by their means, and gives the Wayfarer something to taste [2]. **Shepherds** are also the angels, who act as messengers between God and the Wayfarer, in both directions [3-6].

Those of you who go up refers to those shepherds, desires, who proceed from pure love, since those are the ones who reach God.

The sheepfolds (the shelters of the shepherds with their flock) are the choirs of angels, who sing from choir to choir until they reach God. God is **the hill**, the supreme height.

If by chance you see: you, messenger, if you had the fortune of God accepting to receive, to listen to, the message that you carry on my behalf.

Him I love most: The Wayfarer truly achieves loving God above all things[7] when he reaches the freedom of having complete absence of fear[8-10] and acts only in continual offertory, offering each act to God, sacralising each act, i.e., acting only as a sacrifice[11,12].

Tell him that I am sick, I suffer, and I die: as a lover acting with purity, the Wayfarer does not place a request; he just exposes his need, for the Beloved to act as it pleases Him. Like Mary at the wedding in Canaan, *they don't have wine*[13]. This way of speaking, just indicating his need, without requesting, protects the Wayfarer from egotism, from self-love.

Symbolic translation:

Desires of mine, messenger angels!: those of you, who, because of the purity of love that you come from, do reach the presence of the Supreme, tell Him that I die of need of Him and of suffering, now that I act only as an offering to Him

3

My loves to search for there,
Amongst these mountains and ravines I'll stray,
Nor pluck flowers, nor for fear
Of prowling beasts delay,
But pass through forts and frontiers on my way.

Buscando mis amores
iré por esos montes y riberas;
ni cogeré las flores,
ni temeré las fieras,
y pasaré los fuertes y fronteras.

Seeking my Beloved I will head for those mountains and those watersides; I will neither gather flowers not fear wild beasts; I will go beyond strong men and frontiers.[1]

I will head: With maximum personal effort[2], not just moaning[3]. The Wayfarer knows that prayers and affections are not enough to reach an intimate union with God. He wants to use all possible means. He wants to practice the virtues, exercising himself in the life of contemplative prayer (**mountains**: high and difficult virtues) and in the active life (**watersides**: ascetic mortifications, humble exercises). He will **not gather** (tolerate) **flowers** (delights, consolations in prayer, paranormal powers) [4,5]. He wants to avoid causes of attachments like either material or mental satisfactions, or the spiritual consolations in prayer.

He thus exercises himself in indifference, detachment, observation of the impermanence of all created beings [6-8]. Otherwise, pleasure would take possession of his heart, which the Wayfarer wants to fill with God alone[9].

Nor fear wild beasts: Neither will he tolerate the *enemies of the soul: the Devil, the world and the flesh* [10]. The *Devil*[11] is the **strong men**; *the pleasures of the world* [12] are the **wild beasts**, with power either to cling: friends, social status, material goods; or with power to avert: mockings, absence of spiritual consolations. The **frontiers**, are the obstacles placed by the rebellion of *the flesh* [13,14]: the natural affections and the appetites.

In summary, the method of preparing himself for the journey is the practice of self-knowledge and ascetics: to no longer pursue delights and satisfactions, and to overcome temptations and difficulties through fortitude.

Symbolic translation:

I will practice contemplative love, virtues, humble tasks, and mortifications with the greatest personal effort. I will detach myself from attraction to pleasure and from aversion to displeasure. I will resist temptations and I will direct toward You my affections.

II.

Search for the knowledge of God

After preparing the journey with the practice of the knowledge of one's self (stanzas 1-3) disdaining pleasures, overcoming temptations and difficulties by means of fortitude, the Wayfarer moves now to the search for the knowledge of God by asking

- the irrational creatures (stanzas 4-6)
- the rational creatures (stanzas 7-8)
- the Beloved, requesting Presence and Communion, not just information (stanzas 9-11)

4

The Wayfarer asks the creatures:

> O thickets, densely trammeled,
> Which my love's hand has sown along the height;
> O field of green, enameled
> With blossoms, tell me right
> If he has passed across you in his flight.

> *¡Oh, bosques y espesuras,*
> *plantadas por la mano del amado!*
> *¡Oh prado de verduras,*
> *de flores esmaltado,*
> *decid si por vosotros ha pasado!*

O woods and thickets, planted by the hand of the Beloved ! O green meadow, coated, bright, with flowers: tell me if He has passed by you.[1]

The Wayfarer starts walking along the path that leads to the knowledge of the Beloved by means of the knowledge and consideration of the creatures. He looks at them, watches them, and asks them about Him.

The **woods** represent the whole of the visible Universe.

The **thickets** are the countless living beings that populate earth, seas, and skies.

By the hand indicates that the Beloved created them personally; this observation that it was a *personal* act causes in the Wayfarer a strong awakening to love.

Green meadow refers to Heaven, where nothing fades with time and where the just find eternal joy^2.

Coated, bright, with flowers: beautified with angels and saints.

Tell me if he has passed by you: tell me of the beautiful qualities He has given you.

Symbolic translation:

O whole of the Creation! O all you living beings who populate it, personally created by the Beloved! O angels and saints that adorn Heaven with your presence! Tell me about the beautiful qualities that He has given you, so that I may know Him better.

5

The creatures reply:

> Diffusing showers of grace
> In haste amongst these groves his path he took,
> And only with his face,
> Glancing around the place
> Has clothed them in his beauty with a look.

> *Mil gracias derramando*
> *pasó por estos sotos con presura,*
> *y yéndolos mirando,*
> *con su sola figura*
> *vestidos los dejó de hermosura.*

Pouring out a thousand graces, He passed these groves in haste; and having looked at them, with His image alone, clothed them in beauty.

God left traces of Himself in the creatures by giving them (**pouring**) (1) the *being*, out of the *not-being*, and (2) countless (**a thousand**) **graces** to countless creatures, ordered with a most beautiful interdependence.

He passed, because the creatures are a trace of God's passing. Through them one can track down His wisdom, His grandeur, and various other attributes of Him.

These groves: the elements of which Creation is composed.

In haste, because creation of the creatures is a lesser work compared with what He did with greater attention: the work of the Incarnation of the Word. Only in Jesus shines God with full splendour.

Having looked at them: the book of Genesis 1:31 says: *God looked at all things that he made, and they were good.*

With His image alone, clothed them in beauty: with just the image of His Son, the Word incarnated, He imparted supra-natural being to the human creatures, raising their dignity to that of children of God and clothing them in beauty.

The contemplative praying Wayfarer sees in the creatures all that beauty and all those graces, imparted by God in His own image.

Symbolic translation:

God hastily created countless creatures and gave them innumerable graces. With greater attention He made the works around the Incarnation of the Word, thus vesting humans with the beauty of the dignity of children of God.

6

The Wayfarer speaks:

> O, who my grief can mend!
> Come, make the last surrender that I yearn for,
> And let there be an end
> Of messengers you send
> Who bring me other tidings that I burn for.

> *¡Ay, quién podrá sanarme!*
> *Acaba de entregarte ya de vero.*
> *No quieras enviarme*
> *de hoy más ya mensajero*
> *que no saben decirme lo que quiero.*

Ah, who will have the power to heal me? Surrender Yourself wholly at last. From now on, do not wish to send me any more messengers; they cannot tell me what I wish to hear.

The Wayfarer sees such beauty in the creatures, through which he glimpses traces of the beauty of the Beloved, that he becomes wounded in love, in pain for the lack of plenitude of such love and beauty.

He therefore longs to see the invisible Beauty that created this visible beauty; he says **Ah, who has the power to heal me?** because he does not know how to reach this view of the Beauty and suffers for its absence[1].

He says **surrender yourself wholly now** because the **messengers** (glimpses of the Beloved by means of understanding or feeling or any other communication) increase the hunger for the Beloved and for Beauty, like the small crumbs of bread increase the hunger of the starving one.

Do not send me any more messengers means don't give me any other knowledge [2,3] or any other traces of Yourself, since they only increase my emptiness. Give me direct knowledge of Yourself, immediate, with no mediators. You have shown Yourself to me partially, like at the bottom of fissures in a rock. Show Thyself wholly!

They cannot tell me what I wish to hear means: nothing on Earth or in Heaven can or knows how to show You to me fully. May You, then, be the messenger and the message!

Symbolic translation:

I suffer for not seeing You in full, but through glimpses, emotions, reflections in Your creatures, which show You in a very incomplete way. Show Yourself to me fully!

7

All those that haunt the spot
Recount your charm, and wound me worst of all
Babbling I know not what
Strange rapture, they recall,
Which leaves me stretched and dying where I fall.

Y todos cuantos vagan
de ti me van mil gracias refiriendo,
y todos más me llagan,
y déjame muriendo
un no sé qué que quedan balbuciendo

And all who are wandering free tell me a thousand graceful things of You; all wound me more and leave me dying of, ah, I-don't-know-what, behind their stammering.

All who are wandering free [1]: all who wander in freedom are the rational creatures that use their freedom to choose to go toward God: the angels and saints in their celestial contemplation; human beings, in desiring Him and loving Him.

Tell me a thousand graceful things of You: those who walk knowingly and freely toward God unveil to the Wayfarer, often in a non-verbal way, a knowledge of the Beloved which is higher than the knowledge revealed by the non-rational creatures mentioned in the previous stanza, but still obscure to a certain degree.

The Wayfarer gains from them this knowledge of the Beloved by considering the perfection of those who make such use of their freedom, by the content of their words, and by the secret, non-verbal inspirations whispered to the soul by the Angel Guardian and by other angels.

The Wayfarer says **all wound me more and leave me dying,** because a few brief touches of loving knowledge thus received wound his soul in such a way that they transform it in love[2-4] and, the more love, the greater the blissful pain. The more they talk to him, the more they inspire him to love God more and to know Him more. If that what he understands wounds him of love, what he does not completely understand (but has sublime experience of it), is death for him. It is an impatient love, like the one of Rachel when she says to her husband, Jacob: *give me children, otherwise I will die.*[5]

He says **of, ah, I don't know what**, because this knowledge is unintelligible, indescribable; it refers to the grace and mercy of the Beloved, to countless ineffable secrets; at the same time the Wayfarer knows that there is plenty pending to be revealed to him.

He can't understand these graces, this knowledge, by means of intellectual thinking; it is impossible to express it with human language, and that is why he says **stammering**[6], like children who don't find words to express themselves.

Symbolic translation:

And all of those who, because they are free, choose to move toward Thee, communicate to me a thousand of Thy graces, which are not expressible in human language; they all cause me wounds of love for Thee, and they leave me dying of desire for Thee.

8

How can you thus continue
To live, my life, where your own life is not?
With all the arrows in you
And, like a target, shot
By that which in your breast he has begot.

Mas, ¿cómo perseveras,
¡oh vida!, no viviendo donde vives,
y haciendo porque mueras,
las flechas que recibes,
de lo que del Amado en ti concibes?

How do you endure, O life, not living where you live, and being brought near death by the arrows you receive from that which you conceive of your Beloved?

How do you endure, O life, not living where you live? The soul of the Wayfarer animates his body, but it does not live for the body anymore; in reality it lives, by gift of his love, in his Beloved.

The soul of the Wayfarer asks his bodily life: how can you persevere within this body, for this will delay the true heavenly life in God, in whom (by love, essence and desire) you live more truly than in the body?[1] The Wayfarer suffers for the opposition between those two lives, the natural life of the body and the spiritual life of love. Furthermore, the graces of the love-touches granted to him by the Beloved (**the arrows you receive**) cause him to **conceive of the Beloved** love, grandeur, beauty, wisdom, graces, and virtues, which **have brought you near** in desiring His love.

Symbolic translation:

O life of my soul: how can you endure inside the body, for you live in God by giving Him your love, and His touches, which generate in you such graces and virtues, are in themselves enough to cause you to die of love?

9

Why then did you so pierce
My heart, nor heal it with your touch sublime?
Why, like a robber fierce,
Desert me every time
And not enjoy the plunder of your crime?

¿Por qué, pues has llagado
aqueste corazón, no le sanaste?
Y pues me le has robado,
¿por qué así le dejaste,
y no tomas el robo que robaste?

Why, since You wounded this heart, didn't You heal it? And why, since You stole it from me, did You leave it like this, failing to carry off what You stole?

Why, since You wounded this heart, didn't You heal it? You wounded my heart with the love that resulted from a small, fleeting sight of You and of Your love. Why don't You heal it with the full sight of Your presence, by killing my heart completely with the intensity of your infinite love?

And why, since You stole it from me, did You leave it like this, failing to carry off what You stole? The Wayfarer's complaint is not of the wound, which is sweet, but of the withdrawal of the divine presence, which has left him in a *dark night*, in emptiness, alone, sick, wounded, like a vessel waiting to be filled with water, like a starving person waiting for a crumb of bread, as if he was suspended in the air with nothing to lean on [1]. The Wayfarer experiences his love as emptiness, absence, pain, suffering. At the same time, since his love brings him to giving himself to the Beloved, those feelings are sweet for him. In such circumstances, to reach plenitude of love, a Wayfarer cannot have any desire or hope of reward for his service other than the perfect love of God [2].

The heart stolen by God can be recognized by any of these two signs: (a) if it has longings for God or (b) if it doesn't find satisfaction in anything other than in Him. Love to God can be measured, for it is inversely proportional to self-love, to the importance that the Wayfarer pays to himself. On another hand, the Wayfarer, however great his conformity to the will of the Beloved may be, cannot cease longing for the wages of his love.

Symbolic translation:

Why, after having sweetly wounded me with a spark of Your infinite love, did You retreat and leave me in an empty darkness? Why don't You take me with You?

10

Come, end my sufferings quiet
Since no one else suffices for physician;
And let mine eyes have sight
Of you, who are their light,
Except for whom I scorn the gift of vision.

Apaga mis enojos,
pues que ninguno basta a deshacellos,
y véante mis ojos,
pues eres lumbre dellos,
y sólo para ti quiero tenellos.

Extinguish these miseries of mine, since no one else can stamp them out; and may my eyes behold You, because You are their light, and I would like to open them to You alone[1].

Extinguish these miseries of mine, since no one else can stamp them out: The person sick of love has always his eyes, his attention, fixed on the beloved, even if busy in other deeds; he loses his taste for all other things, and he finds any other deeds burdensome and annoying when he can't see his beloved. The Wayfarer wants to find his Beloved in all things, but he can't find Him in any, and his deeds turn into torments, since they steal him from the peace and quietude of loving contemplation. The fire of love causes him burning sufferings because he experiences his love as *absence* of the Beloved, and he asks Him to extinguish his fire.

May my eyes behold You: only seeing You extinguishes the fire of desire of love for You. God is permanently ready and pays soon a visit to the Wayfarer who has detached himself from all attachments and no longer possesses anything that might withhold him from God.

Because You are their light: Both through the nature of his eyes and through the love of the Wayfarer, his eyes have no other light than You $^{1-4}$. May they see You!

And I would like to open them to You alone: Our faculty to see the divine light is maintained if we don't direct our gaze elsewhere. The Wayfarer who allows maintaining his eyes focused on the light irradiated by something other than God, is looking away from the fountain of the divine light. The spiritual faculty that he has, able to receive God, is then occupied with some other objects and the soul is justly deprived of the divine light. Congruously, the Wayfarer who closes his eyes to all things to open them to God alone, merits his soul to be illuminated by the divine light.

Symbolic translation:

Extinguish the longings and pains of the fire of my love, since only You can do it! May the eyes of my soul behold You face to face, of whom You are their light, and whom I want to possess in order to gaze only at You!

11

Reveal your presence clearly
And kill me with the beauty you uncover,
For pains acquired so dearly
From love, cannot recover,
Save only through the presence of the lover.

Descubre tu presencia,
y máteme tu vista y hermosura;
mira que la dolencia
de amor, que no se cura,
sino con la presencia y la figura.

Reveal Your presence and may the vision of Your beauty be my death; for the sickness of love is not cured except by Your very presence and image[1].

Reveal Your presence: God has certain kinds of hidden presence, where He does not reveal Himself as He is: (1) by essence, in all beings, giving them being and life; (2) by grace, abiding pleased in the soul of those who have not separated themselves from Him by mortal sin. This presence cannot be known by the person who is perfected by it; and (3) by affection, frequent among His devotees, to whom He gives delights and consolations.

The presence that the Wayfarer asks God to reveal for him so that he can see God's divine being, is a *manifest* presence; this happens mainly by means of a certain affective presence given by the Beloved; this type of affective presence is so sublime that the contemplative feels the presence of a being who is immense, hidden, from whom he receives some glimpse of its beauty, with profound effects [2,3]. In summary, the contemplative perceives a supreme good that is present and hidden. The Wayfarer asks here for this perception.

And may the vision of Your beauty be my death: show Yourself to me, even if the full sight of You may not be compatible with life on Earth [4].

For the sickness of love is not cured except by Your very presence and image. The absence of perfect health, due to lack of perfect love, is **the sickness of love**. The more love the person has, the healthier he is, and his sickness is only cured completely when love is complete; that happens when lovers transfigure in one another. True love accepts all that may come from the Beloved (prosperity, adversity, chastisement), for all of that comes from His will.

Symbolic translation:

Uncover Your presence so that I may perceive Your beauty and Your divinity, and may I die for it if it has to be, since my sickness of love for not seeing Your divinity has no other possible cure.

12

O brook of crystal sheen,
Could you but cause, upon your silver fine,
Suddenly to be seen
The eyes for which I pine
Which in my inmost thought my thoughts design!

¡Oh cristalina fuente,
si en esos tus semblantes plateados
formases de repente
los ojos deseados
que tengo en mis entrañas dibujados!

O, spring like crystal! If only, on your silvered-over faces, you would suddenly form the eyes I have desired, which I bear sketched deep within my heart!

The Wayfarer feels that he is quickly coming closer to God, like a stone in free fall, close to touching the ground; he sees himself like moulding wax receiving a preliminary impression of a seal, or like the first sketch of a drawing. He sees his faith increased so as to have a glimpse of the height of God; he suffers because he comes closer to God and has a greater experience within himself of the void of God.

He ardently seeks *union*. He realizes that no help is to be found in the creatures, and he comes back to *faith* as the best vehicle for this *union*. Faith is indeed the only pathway to reach the seventh dwelling place, the *spiritual marriage*[1], the full, permanent *transforming union*.

O, spring like crystal! Faith is the **spring**, since from it flows the water of all spiritual goods[2,3]; it is **like crystal**, since faith is pure, clean, strong.

If only, on your silvered-over faces: faith proposes to us truths of an order higher than the intellectual knowledge of earthly things. To remain in these truths we have to close our intellect to earthly and heavenly things. The substance that faith proposes to us is like gold; it is the Beloved, but faith only reveals truths related to Him and to His presence in an obscure way, half-hidden, as covered by silver. When faith ends due to the direct knowledge, to the clear vision that takes place in the *union*, the silvered cover disappears and gold is uncovered.

You would suddenly form the eyes I have desired: he says **eyes** because he feels a great proximity for the divine truths, the presence of the Beloved, who is gazing at him.

Which I bear sketched deep within my heart: These truths related to the Beloved and to His presence are drawn, **sketched**, not painted in detail, because the Wayfarer knows them imperfectly, he **bears** them **deep within** his **heart**, in the depth of his mind and his soul.

Over this **sketch** drafted by faith, love is formed in the will: the person strengthens his decision to give himself lovingly to the Beloved.

Later in the poem, by means of transformation in love, the Beloved introduces the Wayfarer, by then transformed as His Bride, in His splendour, and full *union* of love takes place: *spiritual marriage, transforming union*. Then this sketch of the Beloved becomes so intimate and vivid that lover and Beloved live in one another, become one another and both become one. Each one gives possession of the self to the other.

Each one lives in the other, each one is the other, and both are one in the transformation of love. St. Paul is transformed in Christ[4]; his life and Christ's life are one, by *union* of love. It is the highest degree of *union*, indescribable[1].

Symbolic translation:

O faith in Christ, my Beloved, of which the spiritual goods flow in a pure, clean, and strong way, if you would only delight in showing me with greater clarity the presence of Him whom I perceive so close to me - presence that you have infused in a dark way in the depth of my soul!

13

Withhold their glance, my Love
For I take wing.
(the Bridegroom:) Turn, Ringdove, and alight
The wounded stag above.
The slope is now in sight
Fanned by the wind and freshness of your flight.

¡Apártalos, Amado,
que voy de vuelo!
(Esposo): Vuélvete, paloma,
que el ciervo vulnerado
por el otero asoma
al aire de tu vuelo, y fresco toma.

Withdraw them, beloved, I am taking flight! (Bridegroom): **Return, dove; the wounded stag is in sight on the hill, cooled by the breeze of your flight**[1].

The beginning of the *spiritual betrothal* is described: God raises the Wayfarer to a high stage of union of love, transient and still not perfect. From here on the Wayfarer is transformed into Betrothed to the Verb, the Son of God. The preparation for perfect *union* in *spiritual marriage* begins.

Withdraw them, beloved, I am taking flight: withdraw Your divine eyes, Beloved, for they take me to a flight of high contemplation where I receive a very high communication and supernatural knowledge; the soul leaves my body, I suffer a great physical torment brought about by these raptures, I feel like a disjointing of the bones, and this seems to me more than what human nature can endure[2].

The Beloved interrupts the flight of the soul with the words: **return, dove**, which is like saying: *dove: return from this high flight of sublime contemplation, ardent love, and simple progress. It is not yet time for you to possess Me fully. Remain with the lower knowledge that I communicate to you in these raptures.*

The wounded stag, which is as if the Beloved was saying: *like the stag, I am also wounded by love when I see your wound of love; if you walk toward Me wounded in love for Me, I also walk toward you, wounded by your wound.*

Is in sight on the hill, which is like saying: *I begin (***in sight***) to reveal Myself to you at the top of the hill, which is the place where the stag likes to go and where I have raised you in your contemplation.*

Cooled is like saying: *Beloved Bride, I am cooled and renewed in the love that arises from your contemplation.* Like a wounded, thirsty stag, the Beloved runs to the fountain of the love professed by the Wayfarer, because one love ignites the other love, and He raises him to be His Bride.

By the breeze of your flight: the **flight** is the ecstasy of this high contemplation; the **breeze** is the pneuma of love and knowledge. Out of this knowledge comes the love by which God communicates and gives Himself. This air or **breeze**, similar to the Holy Spirit who breathes between Father and Son in the Scripture, instructs the soul in its **flight**.

This love is the link of union between soul and God, and between Father and Son. The knowledge is only a source of love. Knowledge without loving self-giving is sterile[3]. God deposits grace and love in the soul just in the measure of its desire and loving self-giving. St. Paul gives a very clear recommendation to grow in love[4].

Symbolic translation:

The Wayfarer, being raised to be the Bride of the Son of God, screams: take away Your divine eyes, Beloved, for they rob me with such impetus and they raise me to a flight of such high contemplation that my human nature can't resist.

The Beloved replies: return from this high flight, beloved, and wait. The sight of your love for Me refreshes Me and wounds Me of love for you. My Spirit already starts revealing itself to you and It starts breathing love to you from the heights where I lift you in contemplation. This communication that you receive is not yet the state of glory that you seek, but rather fleeting glimpses of Myself.

14-15

The Bride:
My Love's the mountain range,
The valleys each with solitary grove,
The islands far and strange,
The streams with sounds that change,
The whistling of the lovesick winds that rove.

Before the dawn comes round
Here is the night, dead-hushed with all its glamours,
The music without sound,
The solitude that clamours,
The supper that revives us and enamours.

Mi Amado, las montañas,
los valles solitarios nemorosos,
las ínsulas extrañas,
los ríos sonorosos,
el silbo de los aires amorosos.

La noche sosegada
en par de los levantes de la aurora,
la música callada,
la soledad sonora,
la cena, que recrea y enamora.

My Beloved, the mountains, and lonely wooded valleys, strange islands, and resounding rivers, the whistling of love-stirring breezes, the tranquil night at the time of the rising dawn, the silent music, the sounding solitude, the supper that refreshes, and deepens love.[1]

After the love flight of the previous stanza (…**I am taking flight…**) the **Beloved** places the Wayfarer in the state of *spiritual betrothal,* with *union* of love, and turns him into His Bride. She has no more laments of love; rather, vested with the graces given by the **Beloved**, she starts a new life of peace, softness, delight, silence, gentleness of love, and she thus sings praises of her new state.

My Beloved: God is, for the Bride, each and every thing cited in these two stanzas, as well as the goodness contained in them. **The mountains and lonely wooded valleys** are big and beautiful, and God is like those for the Bride. She says **strange islands** because in them, like in God, there are new and **strange**[2] things. Like some humans, God is **strange** and superior.

The rivers fill with water every low or empty places; likewise, God fills the soul of the Bride who has lowered herself into nothingness by means of humility, and He fills the places that she had intentionally kept empty for Him every time she denied satisfaction to her appetites to make space for the Beloved.

Resounding: God comes making a clamour that muffles every other sound[3-5]. At the same time, this resounding sound is gentle like the sound of a harp[3].

The whistling [6] is the penetrating and delicate knowledge about God which spills over to the mind, without mediation of the external senses, when God touches the deepest center of the Bride's soul.

The love-stirring breezes are the most joyful feelings that God gives to the Bride during this union. Just as the whistling wind produces touch and sound, these **love-stirring breezes** produce touch (most joyful feelings) and sound (direct knowledge).

She says **the tranquil night** because the **Beloved** is like a tranquil night to the Bride. She sleeps on God's lap in all quietude. This happens **at the time of the rising dawn** because this is not a *dark night* [7] but **a tranquil night** in the quietness of the divine light, in a new knowledge of God that is beginning to come, in which the Bride, in quietude, is being risen to Him from the darkness of the habitual knowledge, sensorial, non-transcendent, to the **rising dawn** of the incipient light of knowledge infused, direct, not mediated by the senses, above all natural understanding, like the awakening from a long sleep with sight of the morning light [8].

She says **silent music** because in this **rising dawn** of **the tranquil night** the Bride realizes the harmony and wisdom of Creation. All creatures raise their voice testifying what God is, each one showing the **Beloved** in their own way, according to what each one of them has received from Him. The **Beloved** has the sweetness of the **music** (symphony of the creatures) and the tranquillity of the quiet, **silent** knowledge.

The **Beloved** is **silent music** (soundless to the senses) and also **sounding solitude**, because the Bride, lacking any other interest, receives with great intensity, **with a loud sound**, the perception of the excellence of God in the creatures.

It is **silent music** and **sounding solitude** because this **music** is only received when there is **solitude** and estrangement from all exterior things[9]. The contradictions contained in the words **silent music** and **sounding solitude** also express the idea that these cannot be perceived by the senses.

The Bride says that this **silent music** and **sounding solitude** are the **Beloved**, God. He is also **the supper that refreshes, and deepens love** because the supper satisfies, refreshes, and gives love, like God does by means of this gentle communication. She says **deepens love** because this is for her like the possession of all goods.

Symbolic translation:

My God, to my eyes You are the Beloved, big, beautiful and solitary like the mountains and the wooded valleys. You show me new things like in an unexplored island. After I humbled myself and denied me of any pleasure so that only You would satisfy me, You do it so loudly that I can't pay attention to anything outside You. You start illuminating me in a very penetrating, delicate, and joyful way while I rest on You with great quietude. You are what satisfies me fully and what fills my soul with love when each creature talks to me about You and all of them join their voices in a tranquil symphony, silent to the senses, perceptible only at the bottom of the soul when I detach my attention from anything created and I remain alone before You.

16

Chase all the foxes hence
Because our vine already flowers apace:
And while with roses dense
Our posy we enlace,
Let no one on the hillside show his face.

Cazadnos las raposas,
que está ya florecida nuestra viña,
en tanto que de rosas
hacemos una piña,
y no parezca nadie en la montiña.

Catch us the foxes, for our vineyard is now in flower, while we fashion a cone of roses intricate as the pine's; and let no one appear on the hill [1]

The Bridegroom pays visits to the Bride, where she habitually enjoys peace and occasionally a very sweet pleasure. At the light that He shines on her, she notices that the virtues (**roses**) are present both in her and in Him. She picks up the virtues and does beautiful acts of love with each one of them and with all of them together (**the vineyard in flower**).

She offers herself and her virtues to Him and He accepts them, with great exchange of love. At this stage the sensory appetites are already at ease, but the Devil disturbs her with the excursions of the imagination and with other knowledges (**the foxes**). The Bride desires this interior enjoyment of love to continue, and she invokes the angels for them to stop (**catch**) these disturbances (**the foxes**).

She says **catch *us***, using the plural, in reference to the Beloved, Who is also present. She says **our**, because the **vineyard**, which is the greenhouse where the virtues grow, is from both of them, Bride and Beloved; it flowers when the Bride employs her will in joining the Beloved and she rejoices in Him by means of all of their virtues. She says **flower** rather than fruit because the latter will be enjoyed in Heaven.

We fashion a cone of roses refers to each virtue being a **rose**, which she and the Bridegroom interweave firmly with the other **roses**, so that each virtue reinforces all others. **While** the virtues (**roses**) are being interwoven, the mind (**the hill**) is more vulnerable to the disturbances (**foxes**). The vulnerability comes from the Bride having emptied herself quite a lot in the spiritual exercise of denying herself of any satisfaction outside the Bridegroom. God has taken her slowly off the dwelling place of the senses, by means of denial (the *dark night*), for her to be able to enter into His garden by means of this interior exercise.

For the perfect enjoyment of this communion, the whole of the mind has to be unoccupied, idle and empty. That is why she says **and let no one appear**, that is, don't let any memory, affection, desire, distraction or fantasy appear before Bride and Bridegroom; let only the will appear and let it occupy itself only in abandonment to the Bridegroom [2].

Symbolic translation:

Oh, Angels, now that my virtues have flowered in the garden I share with the Beloved, and now that He and I reinforce those virtues and interweave them with great exchange of love, chase away any distraction so that I attend only the Beloved by wilfully maintaining my unitive love with Him.

17

Cease, then, you arctic gale,
And come, recalling love, wind of the South.
Within my garden-pale
The scent of flowers exhale
Which my beloved browses with his mouth.

Detente, cierzo muerto;
ven, austro, que recuerdas los amores;
aspira por mi huerto,
y corran sus olores,
y pacerá el Amado entre las flores.

Be still, deadening north wind; south wind, come, you that waken love, breathe through my garden, let its fragrance flow, and the Beloved will feed amid the flowers[1].

The absence of the Beloved in between his visits is incomparably painful and the communication with the creatures is a disturbance. The only desire of the Bride is to please her Beloved with her virtues and for Him to visit her. To prevent the aridity of His absence, the Bride occupies herself in constant devotion and prayer.

The **north wind** brings cold and dryness, while the **south wind** (the

Holy Spirit) brings rain and life. **Be still, deadening north wind** is a plea for the prayer's coldness and dryness to stop. **South wind** (Holy Spirit): **come, you that waken love** between Beloved and Bride. The Holy Spirit wakens up the love that dryness has caused to be half asleep. **My garden** is me; my virtues are the **vineyard in flower** (stanza 16). She does not say *breathe into my garden*, but *breathe **through** my garden*, because she is not asking Him to infuse, *de novo*, virtues and graces; she says **breathe through my garden** because He touches and reinforces virtues and perfections that He had already placed in her. **Breathe through my garden** is the request for a loving visit of the Holy Spirit that will prepare the arrival of the Beloved, the Son of God.

She says **let its fragrance flow** because when the **south wind** of the Holy Spirit stirs up the **garden's** aromatic spices, their scents flare up and **fragrances**, perfections, and virtues that were half asleep, are uncovered, which reveal better the beauty of the Bride. Each of those **fragrances** is invaluable and all of them **flow**, overflow and irradiate an aura of greatness and dignity that inspires respect and awe to everybody around, for their close connection with God. [2, 3]

And the Beloved will feed amid the flowers: The Son of God dwells in her with delight and **feeds** on her, who is seasoned with the spices of the virtues (**the flowers**). He **feeds** on her and on the love grown **amid the flowers** of the virtues and, by **feeding** on her, He transforms her into Himself.

Symbolic translation:

Stop, dryness of prayer and silence of God! Come, Holy Spirit! Awaken the love between my soul and God, which has become sleepy! Renew my virtues and perfections, spread them, and the Son of God will come to feed amid them on my love and on my soul, and we will transform us in one another.

18

O nymphs of Judea,
While yet our flowers and roses
in their flesh hold Ambrosia
Come not here,
But keep the outskirts clear
And do not dare to pass across our threshold!

¡Oh ninfas de Judea,
en tanto que en las flores y rosales
el ámbar perfumea
morá en los arrabales,
y no queráis tocar nuestros umbrales!

O, you nymphs of Judea, while among flowers and rose bushes the amber spreads its perfume, stay away, there on the outskirts; do not so much as seek to touch our thresholds.[1]

The Bride sees the spiritual richness she has acquired; she also sees that the activity of the mind and the outside world disturb the quietness of the noblest center of her soul. God grants her a spiritual delight, but a movement of the mind or an external attraction occurs, and her *union* is disturbed. The Bride, therefore, forbids the thoughts to come close to her[2].

Judea are the senses, which in themselves are blind, as the Judean people are blind regarding our Lord Jesus Christ.

Nymphs are all—outside God—that attract first our intellect (our attention), then our will (calling us for an action). As the **nymphs** attract their lovers, they may attract us by means of the senses, the imagination, or the affections [3].

O, you nymphs of Judea: Oh, you blind movements of the senses, affections, and imagination!

Flowers are the virtues. **Rose bushes are** the mind (intellect and will) in its action of nourishing **the flowers** with the divine concepts (intellect) and acts (will) of self-giving love. **The amber** is the Holy Spirit dwelling in the soul.

While among the flowers and rose bushes the amber spreads its perfume: as long as the Holy Spirit spreads itself in an overflowing way among the virtues and faculties of the Bride.

The outskirts are the periphery of the city; the **city** is the soul. There, **in the outskirts**, dwell the senses, images, and affections (**nymphs of Judea**). If their noise is loud, up-close, within the city, they disturb the communion between God and the center of the soul, where He dwells. For that reason, the Bride commands them to keep quiet:

Do not so much as seek to touch our thresholds: don't even come close to the gate of the town; in other words, not just *don't come in, through the thresholds,* but **don't seek to touch our thresholds**, so as not to distract the quietude of the soul.

Symbolic translation:

Oh, affections, thoughts, appetites, and perceptions of mine! As long as the Holy Spirit spreads itself to overflowing on my soul, stay far away, in silence.

19

Look to the mountain peak,
My darling, and stay hidden from the view,
And do not dare to speak
But watch her retinue
Who sails away to islands strange and new.

Escóndete, carillo
y mira con tu haz a las montañas,
y no quieras decillo;
mas mira las compañas
de la que va por ínsulas extrañas.

Hide Yourself, my love; turn Your face toward the mountains, and do not speak; but look at those companions going with her through strange islands.

Hide Yourself, my love: enter, my Beloved, in the deepest corner (i.e., **hide**) of my soul and reveal to me Your secret wonders. **Your face**: God's face, i.e., the divinity. **Mountains** are the faculties of the mind (intellect and will).

Turn Your face toward the mountains: allow Your divinity to shine into my intellect by giving it divine knowledge and glory and into my will by giving it divine love, so that it will be easier for me to make acts of self-giving love to You[1]. In other words, the Bride is asking for *everything* that she can possibly ask. She does not any more ask for samples, effects of God as in stanza 4 (**tell me, has he passed by You?**), but she rather asks to see His face. This communication occurs with no mediation of the senses, i.e., it is immediate, by means of a direct contact[2]. It is a touch to one another of two naked substances—God and the soul.

And do not speak: carry on communicating with me in this lofty, direct way; not like before when You used to talk to me at a lower level, through the senses and the creatures[3]. **But look**: when God looks, He loves and grants favours[4,5].

At those companions going with her: the **companions** are the virtues, gifts, and perfections that God has given as ornaments to the Bride.

Through strange islands: those companions (virtues, gifts, and perfections) belong to my soul, who goes toward You **through islands** (through pathways and by modes) that are **strange**, foreign to the senses and to any naturally acquired knowledge. Therefore, do allow your communication to be as interior and sublime as to be **strange**, foreign to the senses!

Symbolic translation:

Beloved, enter into the bottom of my soul, love it because of the virtues, gifts, and perfections that You have beautified it with, stay there and continue showing Yourself to me in a sublime and direct way, without mediation of the senses or the natural world!

20- 21

The Bridegroom speaks:

You birds with airy wings,
Lions, and stags, and roebucks leaping light,
Hills, valleys, creeks, and springs,
Waves, winds, and ardours bright,
And things that rule the watches of the night:

By the sweet lyre and call
Of sirens, now I conjure you to cease
Your tumults one and all,
Nor echo on the wall
That she may sleep securely and at peace.

A las aves ligeras,
leones, ciervos, gamos saltadores,
montes, valles, riberas
aguas, aires, ardores
y miedos de las noches veladoras:

Por las amenas liras
y canto de serenas os conjuro
que cesen vuestras iras,
y no toquéis al muro,
porque la esposa duerma más seguro.

Swift-winged birds, lions, stags, leaping roes, mountains, lowlands, and river banks, waters, winds, and ardours, and fears of the watching nights: by the pleasant lyres and the sirens' song, I conjure you to cease your angers and not to touch the wall, that the bride may sleep in deeper peace.[1]

The *spiritual marriage* requires (1) a high degree of purity and (2) firm fortitude. The Bride has to open wide the door of her will and say a complete *yes* so that the Bridegroom may enter in full. This is the *yes* of the *betrothal* before the *marriage*. The Bridegroom will culminate the purification of her soul and grant her a perfect peace. With these stanzas finishes the preparation to the *spiritual marriage*.

The Bridegroom conjures the cease of the lack of ordination in the appetites and in the passions of the Bride, so that the peace of her union to Him not be disturbed. To help her, He communicates and gives Himself to her and proceeds to transform her into Himself.

Swift-winged birds: wanderings of the imagination, swift, restless, that disturb the quietness in which the Bride enjoys the communication from the Beloved. **Lions**: irascibility. **Stags, leaping roes**: appetites, concupiscence. The roe does not only run; he also jumps, motivated by various different stimuli, one after the other. **Mountains, lowlands, river banks** are inordinate acts of the mind (intellect and will) by excess (**mountains**), by defect (**lowlands**), or by slight excess or defect (**river banks**).

Waters, winds, ardours, and fears are the four passions: sorrow, hope, joy, and fear. **Waters**: emotions of sorrow, which enter in the soul like water, covering everything[2]. **Winds**: emotions of hope, which fly to the object hoped for[3]. **Ardours**: joyful emotions, which inflame the heart[4]. **Fears**: in spiritual people, before reaching the *spiritual marriage*, this passion can be intense, sometimes with shivering of the body. **Nights**: the Devil, who induces fears, disseminates darkness and obscures the divine light enjoyed by the Bride.

Watching: because the Devil is always at work and robs the soul the sleep-like peace of her soul. **Lyres:** sweetnesses granted by the Beloved, which give spiritual strength and richness which protect her from the passions reining over her. **Sirens' song**: delights of the union. Just like the sirens in the sea enamour and captivate the sailors with their song, causing them to forget everything else, these sirens absorb the Bride to such a degree that she becomes insensitive to the above disturbances **(birds, lions,** etc.).

I conjure you: I order you with special authority. **Angers**: the shakings of any inordinate passion that cause disquietude to the Bride. **The wall**: the fence of perfections, virtues (**flowers**) and peace that protects the garden reserved for the Beloved[5]. The Bride is in this garden, and He **feeds among the flowers** (among her virtues, see stanza 17)

That the bride may sleep in deeper peace: the Spouse will now be able to take delight in the gentle sleep of quietude and sweetness that she enjoys in her *union* with the Beloved[6]. None of her doors is closed, but she has now the freedom needed to enjoy this union. She has withdrawn of all created things and nothing may disturb her[7]. She possesses such grandeur and stability that she lacks feelings of sorrow due to sin, or of compassion due to acts of mercy. There is nothing for her to desire or to hope for. No emotion of joy causes her any desire to possess or to have greater abundance.

She has perfect awareness, satisfaction, and delight in the fullness of God's riches, which are hers, and any new, accidental joy or satisfaction is comparatively insignificant. She does not receive new delights, but she delights anew in those that she already possesses. It is like the sea, which, at sunrise, shines on depths and caves with pearls and veins of gold that were already there, but at the sunlight receive a more admirable appearance[8]. The Spouse has entered in God, where she enjoys a *peace* and delight *that surpasses all understanding*[9]. In her, leaps the fountain of *living water* that gives *life everlasting*[10]. She has been transformed and has grown to her full stature. In front of life or death she is in conformity with the will of God and, without any impulse of longing or appetite, she says with simplicity: *thy will be done*[11,12].

Symbolic Translation:

Thoughts, emotions, perceptions, and passions of My beloved Bride: by the sweetnesses and delights that she experiences in her union with Me, I conjure you to stop disturbing her with your intemperances, so that she may maintain this union with Me!

III.

Spiritual Marriage, Unitive Way, Transforming Union

The Wayfarer has walked along the *Purgative Way* (stanzas 1- 5) and has exercised himself in mortification and discursive meditation (stanzas 1-2). With stanza 13 (**Withhold their glance, my Love**) starts the *Betrothal, Contemplative or Illuminative Way*. Along this way, with great effort, the Bride calms the imaginations and appetites (**catch the foxes**, stanza 16), overcomes the dryness of prayer (**stops the northern wind**, stanza 17), calms the blind movements of the senses, imagination, and affection (**nymphs of Judea**, stanza 18), all of which are obstacles to the *spiritual marriage*, and obtains the Holy Spirit (**south wind**, stanza 17) that allows her to prepare and perfect the *spiritual marriage*.

The description of the *Spiritual Marriage, Unitive Way or Transforming Union* starts with stanza 22. As the Spouse advances along this path, her soul becomes perfect in loving Him by means of the *spiritual marriage*. The union is full, perfect. Each one of them gives itself completely to the other with consummation in the union of love. The soul is transformed in divine. This is the highest possible stage on Earth. It is similar to the union of the light of a candle with the light of the sun. The latter has absorbed into its light the light of the former.

Stanza 22 is the synthesis of the *unitive way*. This *way* is explained in greater detail in stanzas 26-30: gifts to the Spouse when she gives herself to Him (stanzas 26- 27). Gift of love: love as the highest personal achievement (stanza 28). Gift of love: love as the highest form of service to the Church (stanza 29). Bridegroom and Bride working as one single being (stanza 30).

22

The Bridegroom speaks:

> Now, as she long aspired,
> Into the garden comes the bride, a guest;
> And in its shade retired
> Has leant her neck to rest
> Against the gentle arm of the Desired.

> *Entrádose ha la esposa*
> *en el ameno huerto deseado*
> *y a su sabor reposa*
> *el cuello reclinado*
> *sobre los dulces brazos del amado.*

The bride has entered the sweet garden of her desire and she rests in delight laying her neck on the gentle arms of her beloved.[1]

To reach this point of union with her Bridegroom, in freedom, the Wayfarer has worked hard in his search for Him, has given himself in *betrothal* and has been finally lifted to her *spiritual marriage*.

In this stanza, however, we see that He was seeking her even more and it was actually she, not Him, the one who was hiding outside the **garden**

[2,3]. The Good Shepherd holds on his shoulders the lost sheep for which he had searched along many winding paths[4]. The Housewife, after having lit a candle and hunting through Her whole house, finds the drachma (*the bride*) that She had lost, holds it up in Her hands with gladness and calls Her friends and neighbours to come, celebrate and rejoice with Her that She finally found it [5]; the King asks all of His angels and saints—calling them *daughters of Zion*—to share in His gladness and calls the Wayfarer His crown, His bride, and the joy of His heart [6].

This loving Shepherd, Housewife, King and Bridegroom, rejoices that the Wayfarer has become free and He carries this rescued, perfected soul on His shoulders, held by His hands in this union that He so much desired. He takes her then in His **arms** and goes forth with her as the Bridegroom from his bridal chamber.[7]

He declares, thus, that the Wayfarer has achieved victory, has reached the state of *spiritual marriage*, and He mentions properties of this state: to **rest in delight** and to **lay her neck**.

The bride has entered indicates that she has abandoned *everything* temporal and material: affections, temptations, inconveniences, pains, cares.

The sweet garden is God. She is now transformed in Him. This union is beyond words and thoughts. He is for her a **sweet and desirable garden** for it has mature fruits and flowers, ready for the Spouse. This state is incomparably safer, more stable, pleasant and with peace, than the *betrothal*. It is as if her existence would since only occur in the **arms** of the Beloved. Since she is completely united with God, her life is as pleasant as God's life and she is not capable of feeling or perceiving anything unpleasant because she experiences and enjoys the glory of God in her own soul, which has been transformed in Him. **In delight**: fully pleased.

Rests indicates that she used to work hard to perfect herself, in her battle to conquer the virtues. Now she just **rests. The gentle arms of her beloved** represent the strength of God, which is gentleness for her. **Her neck** represents her strength, which makes her union with God possible. If she were not strong, she could not resist such an intimate embrace. Just like a bride has a certain physical strength on her own, but it turns into weakness when she is embraced by the bridegroom, similarly, what used to be strength of the Spouse (**her neck**) becomes weakness once she is on His arms

Laying her neck on the gentle arms of her beloved means for the Spouse to have her weakness now united to the strength (**the arms**) of God. Now God is the strength and sweetness of the Spouse, in which she is now sheltered, protected from any evil and enjoying all goods. In the union, the soul kisses God without paying attention or being distracted by anything or anybody. Neither the Devil nor the world nor the flesh disturb her. *Winter is now past, the rains gone, and the flowers have appeared in our land.* [8]

Symbolic translation:

The Bride, strengthened, has abandoned all cares and creatures, and has entered within Me. She is now My Spouse; fully joyful, she rests, entrusting her weakness to My omnipotence.

23

Beneath the apple tree,
You came to swear your troth and to be mated
Gave there your hand to me,
And have been new-created
There where your mother first was violated.

Debajo del manzano
allí conmigo fuiste desposada.
Allí te di la mano
y fuiste reparada
donde tu madre fuera violada.

Beneath the apple tree, there I took you as My spouse; there I gave you My hand and restored you, where your mother had been corrupted[1].

Beneath the apple tree: beneath the divine gift of the wood of the Cross (**the apple tree**) the Son of God redeemed and espoused human nature, and gave each person the grace and the promises needed for the full *spiritual marriage* with Himself.

There I took you as My spouse: there I gave you the graces needed for you to unite yourself fully with Me as My Spouse and companion.

There I gave you my hand: there I offered you My loving consideration and My assistance, raising you from your lowly state to be a *child of God*.

And restored you where your mother was corrupted: your human nature (**your mother**) was **corrupted** in your First Parents and you were later **restored beneath the** tree of the Cross (**apple tree**). Your mother brought you death under the tree in the Garden of Eden (**apple tree**)[2] and I brought you life under the tree of the Cross (**apple tree**).

Symbolic translation:

Under the Cross I repaired the nature that you had in a corrupt state due to your First Parents and I gave you My loving consideration and the necessary graces for your full union with Me.

24

The Bride speaks:

Now flowers the marriage bed
With dens of lions fortified around it,
With tent of purple spread,
In peace securely founded,
And by a thousand shields of gold surmounted.

Nuestro lecho florido,
de cuevas de leones enlazado,
en púrpura tendido,
de paz edificado,
de mil escudos de oro coronado.

Our flowered bed, bound round with linking dens of lions, hung with purple, built up with peace, and crowned with a thousand shields of gold. [1-3]

The **bed** of the Spouse is the Beloved, the Son of God, in whom she reclines by means of union of love. **Flowered** refers to the Beloved, the Verb, because He is the very *flower of the fields and lily of the valleys* [4], flowered for her, full of fragrance and beauty. The **flowered bed** is delectable, for now that she has become His Spouse, she has united herself to Him and reclines in Him; He gives her wisdom, secrets, graces, virtues and makes her thus incomparably rich and beautiful.

For that reason she also calls **flowered bed** her union with Him. She says **our** because both He and she have the same virtues and the same love: that of Him. In this state her virtues are now perfect and heroic, **flowered**. These virtues do not act all at once, but remain latent, waiting for their chance, although the Spouse never lacks the peace and quietude that they provide her with.

Each virtue that the Spouse possesses in this state of union is like a **den** where Christ, united with the soul in that virtue and in all other virtues, dwells and helps her like a **lion**. In this way all virtues remain safeguarded, protected against any beast, which dares not to come close. The Spouse, united with God in those same virtues, is also like a **lion**, because she receives His same properties.

She says **bound round with linking dens** because in this state, for a more complete perfection of the Spouse, the virtues complement one another without leaving any weakness in between them. They are all tightly **linked, bound round** and nothing in the world can even move the Spouse. Free from any disturbance of the natural passions, naked of any temporal care, she enjoys her sharing of God in peace and safety. The soul becomes equal to God through love. She never loses any peace or sweetness.

This **flowered bed**, which is for her the bed of transformation in God through union of love, is thus perfectly protected by the **linking** of virtues strengthened by the Beloved, the **dens of lions bound round.**

Purple is the color of the king's robes and the colour of charity in the Scriptures. The **flowering bed** is **hung with purple** because all the virtues and riches are sustained and flowered only by the charity of the Heavenly King [3]. These virtues and riches **hang** from God by means of His **purple coloured** charity. In all things and actions these virtues and riches move the Spouse in a **purple-**coloured, charitable and loving way to a greater love to God.

The **bed is built up with peace**: the union (the bed) with the Beloved produces in the Spouse effects of **peace**, meekness, and fortitude. The Spouse is so quiet and secure that she seems to be **built up of peace**. Each of the many (**thousand**) virtues and gifts of the Spouse is a **shield**. They **crown** her as a reward for her battles to acquire them. They are of a high value (**of gold**) in the defence against vices.

Symbolic meaning:

I am reclined with Christ, Heavenly King, who is Beauty itself, in union of love, on a bed of charity that is He Himself. By His love He rewards my former efforts by pouring on me and sharing with me countless graces and His own virtues, protected by Himself. These complement and strengthen one another; they are perfected to a heroic degree and they protect me against vices. He dwells in each one of them and they transform me, through love, in a person made of immutable peace.

25

Tracking your sandal-mark
The maidens search the roadway for your sign,
Yearning to catch the spark
And taste the scented wine
Which emanates a balm that is divine.

A zaga de tu huella
las jovenes discurren al camino,
al toque de centella,
al adobado vino,
emisiones de bálsamo divino.

Following Your footprints, maidens walk along the way; the touch of a spark, the spiced wine, cause flowings in them from the balsam of God[1-4].

The Bride speaks here of three types of delights and favours received while walking toward God: **Footprints, touch of sparks, and spiced wine.**

Footprints are the sweetness and knowledge of God left in the soul of those who search for Him, which others notice and may use to track down God and follow Him. This is the main mode that God uses to attract Wayfarers.

The touch of sparks shot by the divine love are perceived as subtle unexpected touches that suddenly inflame the Wayfarer in a fire of feelings of love. They happen unexpectedly, while on any activity, and they are brief and intense, although their effect may last a long time[5]. The type of **touch** varies from person to person according to their degree of perfection. Sometimes this **spark** leaves the soul burning in intense love for a long time. Those who are relatively new in serious practice of prayer and receive these **sparks** may act with great fervour initially, but they may soon lose their perseverance if they lose that fire. These sparks cause a *feeling* of love, perceptible, superficial. Those who have been loving for a longer time, process love in a more stable way by means of self-giving and good works, rather than by ardent fervour. These lack, therefore, the anxieties and afflictions of the feelings of love. The Bride in the Song of Songs mentions allegorically these **sparks**.[4]

The spiced wine is an abundance of love that God infuses to more perfect people, inebriating them with the Holy Spirit with a reinforced, **spiced** wine of sweet love, which causes lifting of the spirit and bursts of love, praise and reverence, with great desires to work and to suffer for Him. It has a long duration, sometimes several days, spontaneously rising and lowering in intensity. The Wayfarer, without doing anything on his own, feels in his most intimate center that his soul is being inebriated and inflamed by this feeling of divine love. [6]

The maidens are other Wayfarers that go toward God, mentioned now by the Spouse, who have seen the **footprints** of the Bridegroom and who feel the **touches of sparks** and **the spiced wine**.

Run along the way of life everlasting and evangelical perfection (sanctity, poverty, chastity, obedience) by means of works, prayer, and external practices, to end up meeting the Beloved in union of love after denuding themselves of any possession, attachment or bond to any creature. They **run** this **way** in countless different modes, according to what God gives to each one of them, with great differences in works and spiritual practices.[7]

Balsam of God is the divine love—love from the Wayfarer toward God and love from God toward the Wayfarer. From the side of the Wayfarer, the **flowings from the balsam of God** are movements and voluntary acts from himself toward God by means of acts of loving, giving, reverence, thankfulness, prayer, desire, and delight in the taste of love. From the side of God, His **balsam** comforts and heals the Wayfarer by its fragrance and its medicinal effects. The **spiced wine** and the **touch of the spark** are **flowings from this balsam of God**.

Symbolic translation:

The Wayfarers who walk toward You guide themselves by the sweetness and wisdom they see in themselves and in others who also walk toward You. Sometimes they receive unexpected bursts of feelings of Your love, fleeting and intense; at some other times, when they are closer to You, an intense and prolonged inebriation of You falls upon them. All of that stimulates them to aim at You their feelings and works of love and praise.

26

Deep-cellared is the cavern
Of my loves heart, I drank of him alive;
Now, stumbling from the tavern,
No thoughts of mine survive,
And I have lost the flock I used to drive.

En la interior bodega
de mi amado bebí, y cuando salía
por toda aquesta vega
ya cosa no sabía
y el ganado perdí, que antes seguía.

In the inner wine cellar I drank of my Beloved and, when I went abroad through all this valley, I no longer knew anything, and lost the herd which I was following.[1]

The Spouse narrates the sovereign favour made by God, Whom, by recollecting her in the intimacy of His love, transformed her in Himself by union or transformation of love. She mentions the effects of this union: forgetfulness and withdrawal of all what is worldly, and mortification (actively inducing the death) of all of her appetites and gratifications.

The inner wine cellar is the last, most intimate (**inner**) degree of love and union that can occur in this life, the *spiritual marriage*, the Seventh Dwelling Place of St. Teresa of Jesus[2]. Many people enter the first wine cellars, but few reach the **innermost** one, the **wine cellar** of the *spiritual marriage*. What God communicates here is completely beyond words. Nothing can be said about it, just like nothing can be said about God that resembles God. It can only be said: **I drank of my Beloved**.

As the wine of love that God gives in this stage diffuses through the veins and through the body, the soul becomes transformed in God. Both become one, like the window glass, bathed by the sunlight, becomes light. The most intimate part of the Spouse remains from now on permanently in a state of conscious union with God, but her intellect and her will may take part in other activities. **And, when I went abroad** refers to the time periods where the intellect, unable to remain in uninterrupted and permanent union, intermittently leaves and enters this state of union.

Through all this valley: throughout the vast world. **I no longer knew anything**: in this state of highest union the Spouse is being informed with supernatural knowledge, at whose presence all other prior knowledge shows to be ignorance[3,4]. The full immersion in God, by which the Spouse is absorbed in the love, causes her to become annihilated in regards to all things and to herself, as if she had vanished and dissolved in love, moving from herself to the Beloved. The Spouse becomes unable of perceiving evil in evil things, because evil has disappeared from her.[5]

She says **I no longer knew anything** because she ignores, she has no interest, in any other business. She no longer needs to understand the things she used to attend; it is as if the light of the sun had been added up to the old candle of her soul. She is no longer aware of herself. She only sees the love she drinks, she becomes pure and simple like God, and stays radiant in simple contemplation. This big beam of love annihilates all that was not love in her.

And lost the herd which I was following refers to the fact that prior to this state of highest union there were still some residue of appetite and desire, natural or spiritual, that she would seek and tried to satisfy: desire to know things; to receive small gratifications; attachment to some little possession, to one object more than to another, to some particular food or drink, to the desire of spiritual satisfactions, to pleasant memories. She no longer occupies herself in following thoughts caused by any of the four passions of her soul: joy, hope, fear, sorrow.

Symbolic translation:

At the highest and most intimate degree of union of love, I drank love from my Beloved, I became transformed in Him, I became permanently united with Him and whenever my intellect transiently left this state of union, all across the world I saw nothing but God in everything and I did not have any more clinging, aversion, or desire to anything.

27

He gave his breast, seraphic
In savor was the science that he taught;
And there I made my traffic
Of all, withholding naught,
And promised to become the bride he sought.

Allí me dio su pecho
allí me enseñó ciencia muy sabrosa
y yo le di, de hecho,
a mí, sin dejar cosa.
Allí le prometí de ser su esposa.

There He gave me His breast; there He taught me a sweet and living knowledge; and I gave myself to Him, keeping nothing back; there I promised to be His spouse.[1,2]

In this union God communicates Himself to the Spouse with such genuine love that the loves of a mother, sibling or friend can't compare with it. God loves in such a degree of humility and sweetness, that the Father exalts the Spouse as if He was her servant, or as if He was the mother nursing her baby[3]. The Spouse becomes so melted by His love, that she gives Him all of her will and love[2]. This mutual surrender is so complete, that she says **There He gave me his breast; there He taught** me a sweet and living knowledge; and I gave myself to Him, keeping nothing back; there I promised to be His spouse.

Giving His breast to one another means giving love and revealing secrets to one another.

There He taught me a sweet and living knowledge refers to the science of contemplation, the *mystical theology*, which is the knowledge obtained by means of love. It is scientific **knowledge**, because it is both perceived and verifiable by the intellect, and it is **sweet,** because it is communicated in love.

And I gave myself to Him, keeping nothing back indicates that she gives herself to Him wholly, with the desire not to possess anything ever again for herself. In this union God gives her the purity and perfection that she needs for such surrender; He transforms her into Himself, He takes full possession of her and He empties her of all that she possesses, except of Himself. She gives herself wholly to God, not only in her will but also in her actions, without keeping anything, just like God has given Himself freely to her. The will of both is mutually given and satisfied, with the fidelity and stability of an espousal.

There I promised to be His spouse: just as in ordinary married life the spouse only loves, cares, and works for her husband, in *spiritual marriage* the Spouse has all of her affections, knowledge, cares, appetites and works, all entirely inclined to God. She is so directed toward God[4] that even her first inclinations, the first movements of her attention, occur only in conformity to the will of God. The Wayfarer who has reached this state of *spiritual marriage* now only knows to love and to walk with her Beloved in the delights of their love. The Wayfarer has reached perfection, whose form and nature are love[5]; the more a person loves, the more completely she loves, and therefore this Spouse that is now perfect, is in its being only love, and all of her acts are acts of love.

She has found the treasure of love, hidden in God, and she only employs all of her faculties and possessions in loving, abandoning everything else[6]. She is aware that He values love so much that He does not care or uses anything else but love, and for this reason she employs all of her strength in pure love to God, wishing to serve Him perfectly. She works in such a way not only because He desires it so, but also because the love that unites her to Him moves her to love Him in all things and by means of all things. Just as the bee finds many flowers along her way, she extracts honey from all of them, and does not use them for anything else, similarly the Spouse extracts easily the sweetness of love from all that happens to her. She loves God in everything; everything leads her to love and she does not know anything other than love. That is why she exclaims in the next stanza: **…for now my every act is love.**

Symbolic translation:

There He gave me His love and, by means of His love, He made Himself known to me. There I gave Him all of my desires, my works, my future and my whole being, promising myself to Him as His spouse.

28

Now I occupy my soul
and all my energy in his service;
I no longer tend the herd,
nor have I any other work
now that my every act is love.

Mi alma se ha empleado,
y todo su caudal en su servicio:
ya no guardo ganado,
ni ya tengo otro oficio,
que ya sólo en amar es mi ejercicio.

Now I occupy my soul and all my energy in His service; I no longer tend the herd, nor have I any other work, for now my every act is love.[1]

Love has the property of making the lover equal to the beloved object. In the state described in this stanza, the Wayfarer possesses perfect love and has become *Spouse of the Son of God*, which implies equality with Him and sharing His possessions. The Spouse explains now how she brings about her surrender to her Bridegroom:

Now I occupy my soul: she has abandoned herself to the Beloved in this union of love in which she now occupies **all my energy**: the intellect in understanding, the will in acting with surrender, thus attaching love to all things; the passions (joy, hope, fear, sorrow) all refer now to the Beloved; the gifts and skills, only at His service; **all**, from the first inclination of any thoughts and desires whatsoever until the completion of any action, **in his service**, i.e., placed only at His service.[2]

One of the consequences of the Spouse **occupying all** of her **energy** in His service is that she, accustomed to working only for God, tends to forget that she is working for Him and does it by habit, without thinking on it. **I no longer tend the herd** means: I no longer seek pleasures or satisfaction of my appetites. **Nor have I any other work**: I no longer distract myself with useless occupations, in other words, foreign to the development of love[3], nor with occupations directed to my own satisfaction or to please others (compliments, human respects).

For now my every act is love: I no longer have any mode of acting other than the exercise of love, for I have changed to **loving** all of my previous ways of relating to God. All I do I do it with love; since I accept unconditionally all that happens to me as coming from the will of God, all I suffer I suffer with the delight of loving, and all I do or experience causes in me a rise in love and a delight in God. Even praying, where I used to reflect and dialogue is now exclusively an exercise of love[4]. This is a love of the whole being, with the whole of her existence and her actions, not just an effusion of a feeling. In this state of *spiritual espousal*, **the person walks with God in union of love, which is a habitual and loving attention to His will.**

Symbolic translation:

I have surrendered myself to You; the whole of my being is now placed exclusively at Your service. I no longer go about seeking satisfactions for myself or for others; I don't get distracted with occupations or pastimes foreign to the growth of love. I have changed all other previous modes of relating to You or to others. My new and only way is *loving You.*

29

So now if from this day
I am not found among the haunts of men,
Say that I went astray
Love-stricken from my way,
That I was lost, but have been found again.

Pues ya si en el ejido
de hoy más no fuere vista ni hallada,
direis que me he perdido;
que andando enamorada,
Me hice perdidiza y fui ganada.

If then, I am no longer seen or found on the common, you will say that I am lost; that, stricken by love, I intentionally lost myself, and was gained.

The Spouse withdraws from everything related to the active life, to devote herself only to what the Beloved says is the only thing necessary[1], which is: **attentiveness to God and continuous exercise of a loving offer to Him.**

The **common** is the place at the exit of the village where people meet to enjoy themselves and have fun, and where the shepherds bring their herds. By **common** the Wayfarer refers to the world, where people entertain themselves with pastimes and with conversations foreign to the growth in love, and where people nourish their appetites.

The Spouse proclaims and glories herself in having lost both the world and her own for the Beloved: **If then, I am no longer seen or found on the common, you will say that I am lost.** She explains that if she is **no longer seen or found** occupied in her previous worldly activities, people should believe and declare that she is **lost** for all creatures; these can't find her any more.

I lost myself: she has withdrawn from all of that; she no longer pays attention to the business of the creatures, but only to those of the Beloved.

At the beginning of the spiritual life, the Wayfarer has to exercise love both in the active and in the contemplative way, behaving both like Martha and like Mary[1]. However, once this state of union of love is reached, she ought not to get involved in any work whatsoever that could present the slightest obstacle to the loving attentiveness to God, even if such work was of great service to God, because even a small amount of this pure love is more precious to God and to the soul and more beneficial to the Church than all those other works together, even if it appears that nothing is being done. **This love is the end for which we have been created.**

Before reaching the state of *spiritual espousal*, the works done for love of Christ are not carried out with perfection and nakedness of spirit; it is generally pondered *what will others say* or *how will the work look like*; there are two interests, two masters, and inevitably the Bride will fail to one of them [2]. The Spouse declares that, in order not to fail God, she failed to all that is not God (to herself and to all other creatures), losing everything for love to Him.

That, stricken by love, I lost myself: anybody truly in love leaves everything to come closer to his beloved. The Spouse has abandoned everything; conquered by love, she does not occupy her spirit in anything other than *attentiveness to God and continuous exercise of love to Him.* She has wilfully lost herself, by means of not paying any attention to herself, concentrating herself in the Beloved and abandoning herself to Him freely and selflessly, with no desire to gain anything for herself.

And was gained: she accounts this loss as a great good that she desired; for her, her loss was her gain, and that is why she lost herself wilfully. The desire to be **gained** was the reason leading her to abandon everything, to **lose herself.** He who walks in the love of God does not seek gain or reward, but only to detach himself voluntarily of all things and to lose himself for God, and he judges this loss to be a gain of all things and of himself. That is why she says **and was gained**. When the Wayfarer has reached such point where he no longer looks for God in considerations, shapes, forms, feelings or by means of creatures or of the senses, but has advanced beyond all of these and beyond all ways and manners, and simply enjoys communion with God in faith and in love, it is said that God is her gain because she has lost all that is not God and has gained God.

Symbolic translation:

If then I am never again seen in public or enjoying myself, you will say that, having fallen in love with God, I abandoned everything and I gained Him.

30

Of flowers and emeralds sheen,
Collected when the dews of dawning shine,
A wreath of garlands green
(That flower for you) will twine
Together with a golden hair of mine.

De flores y esmeraldas
en las frescas mañanas escogidas
haremos las guirnaldas
en tu amor florecidas
y en un cabello mío entretejidas.

With flowers and emeralds chosen on cool mornings we shall weave garlands flowering in your love, and bound with one hair of mine.[1,2]

The interior exchanges between God and the Spouse are ineffable because of their delicate and sublime character. In ordinary life the bride, on the day of the espousal, understands only about what pertains to the delicacy of their love and to the uncovering of all of her virtues and jewels intended to please the bridegroom. He acts similarly, granting her graces and showing her all of his richness to console her and to give happiness to her. The virtues and graces of both of them come to light and both show them to one another to celebrate the feast of their espousal. In the mystical espousal of the Wayfarer who has been transformed into the Spouse, she sings to the Bridegroom the goods and delights that both exchange with one another.

Flowers are the perfect virtues of the Spouse. **Emeralds** are the gifts, the graces received from God. The **cool mornings** are the acts of love and the efforts made at times of dryness and spiritual difficulty, since in those circumstances the virtue becomes more stable than when obtained in spiritual delights [3]. **Cool mornings** refers also to the youth, which is the age most pleasant to God to choose virtues, because it is then that the vices oppose the virtues with greatest strength.

Chosen: these virtues were selected instead of their opposing vices. Also, only the most perfect virtues were chosen among all virtues. **Chosen on cool mornings** emphasizes the excellence, the perfection of the virtues (**flowers**) to be interwoven with the **emeralds** (gifts from God, graces).

We shall weave means that we will enjoy them together, working together the Spouse and God as a team[4]. Neither the Spouse can acquire the virtues without the help of God, nor can God imprint them in the Spouse without her help. The virtues in the Spouse are beautified in the love that He has toward her and they are maintained by the love she has for Him.

Garlands indicate the perfection of the Spouse; it also refers to all of the Wayfarers sanctified by Christ in the Church, and to the aureoles made by Christ and by the Church with white flowers (virgins), resplendent flowers (holy doctors) and with crimson carnations (martyrs).

When the virtues (**flowers**) and graces (**emeralds**) have been obtained in a complete degree, the **garland** of the perfection of the Spouse is complete; in other words, she is vested of perfect love and surrounded with a great variety of perfect virtues and graces, so that she can now present herself to the King with dignity [5].

Flowering in your love: the love that God pours onto the Spouse gives grace and power to her works, allowing them to flourish. Without this love the works could be perfect from a human viewpoint, but would wither and lack any value at the eyes of God. Since God bestows His grace and love on them, the works of the Spouse are now blossomed in His love.

These **garlands** that God and the Spouse **weave** when they **choose** and exchange virtues, graces, and acts of love (**flowers and emeralds**), they are being **bound**, i.e., they are being firmly attached upon the Spouse. At the end of this process, the perfection of the Spouse is complete: the Wayfarer has reached the state of *perfection*.

The **hair** is the love of the Spouse, whose will directs it to the Beloved. It is the thread of the **garland**. This thread of love, this **hair, binds** and sustains the virtues to the Spouse by means of the will; should the love break because of an offense to God, the virtues would fall off, as would happen to the flowers of a garland should its thread break. It is not enough for God to love us and to give us virtues; in order to be able to receive them and to preserve them, we, too, have to use our will to love Him with our actions.

The Spouse uses just **one hair**, not many, because her will has just **one** objective, separated from any other hair of the will where she could interweave some other little love or appetite. She emphasizes the value of the **garlands** because when love is fixed solely and firmly in God, as she says, the virtues are also perfectly, completely, and full-**flowering** in the love of God. By their own essence, by that which is most intimate and authentic to them, the **flowers** (virtues) and **emeralds** (gifts received from God) **bound,** give to the Spouse a strength and majesty that make her impermeable to the penetration of ugliness or imperfections, and vest her with ineffable loveliness and charm.

Symbolic translation:

Between the two of us we will make my soul perfect by firmly fixing on it both my best virtues, obtained with effort by means of my difficult acts of love, as well as by the graces granted by You. I remain perfect thanks to directing my love and my will only to You. Your love to me will make these virtues bear fruit in my works of love.

31

One hair (upon my nape
You loved to watch it flutter, fall and rise)
Preventing your escape,
Has snared you for a price
And held you, to be wounded from my eyes.

En solo aquel cabello
que en mi cuello volar consideraste,
mirástele en mi cuello
y en él preso quedaste
y en uno de mis ojos te llagaste.

You considered that one hair fluttering at my neck; You gazed at it upon my neck and You became its captive; and You became wounded by one of my eyes.[1]

In this stanza the Spouse wants to describe the *union of love*. Love is not a feeling that effuses, but an act, a manifestation of the will.

The **hair** is the love of the Spouse, only **one**, not sheared with any other creature.[2] She directs her will only toward the Bridegroom, thus binding and interweaving her virtues, the **flowers**, among one another. This hair of love also unites[3] her soul with the Flower of flowers[4]. The

Spouse resembles the perfect Flower by the perfection and beauty of each of her own **flowers** (virtues). This **hair** of love between God and the Spouse is of such strength as to transform them and unite them with such grandeur that, while different in substance, the soul of the Spouse and God resemble one another in glory and appearance. On His side, God is neither still nor waiting for the Spouse, but is the main lover and principal performer; He is also the **hair** (love) that unites Him with her, since this **hair** penetrates both of them with strength.

My neck is the strength, purity, and integrity of my faith and of my love. The interweaving of the virtues is as strong as a **neck** that no vice opposed to the virtues of the **garlands of flowers** could break. God especially values the strength (**neck**) of love, i.e., the laborious acts of love.

In this stanza it is as if she said: *You loved me when You saw my strength.* Previously God had seen her will and love (**hair**) bound with ropes[5], attached to other affections, pleasures and appetites; it was not **fluttering**, not alone (**one**), it had no strength (**neck**). However, once the Bride has become so detached and strong by means of mortifications and penances, her love becomes like the love of the Spouse of Christ, so strong that no force or occasion can break it any longer.

The breeze of the Holy Spirit[6] carries swiftly, **fluttering, the hair** of love of the Spouse to God, with strength (**at my neck**), without going astray for anything or for anybody.

You considered: You gazed very particularly, with attention and with esteem, at my **hair** (love); You saw that it was alone, **one;** You saw its strength (**neck**); and You saw it **fluttering** toward You, carried by the Holy Spirit. The words **you considered** point out also how much God cherishes a strong love, a love expressed with laborious acts. To emphasize this cheer she repeats the word **neck** (strength).

The consideration of the strength of my love pleased You and urged You to move Your eyes and to pleasingly gaze at this **hair** of mine. For God, to **gaze** is to love[7]. God descended to this world [8-15] to gaze at us, to wake up the fluttering of our love and to give us courage to fly[16].

God now **gazes at** the love of the Spouse, takes the **flowers and emeralds of the garlands,** and He interweaves them with Himself. The Spouse has achieved a great detachment, her hair of love is now **one**, alone; she has now enough strength to keep the virtues anchored to her soul and she now deserves *union*. Upon gazing at her and seeing all of that, God **became captive** by the **hair**, in the love of the Spouse. The captivity of the Creator upon seeing the little love for Him by a creature resembles the eagle that descends from the heights with the desire to be captivated, and is captured by a little bird of lowly flight. God, thus, becomes captive by a hair! The Spouse finds unspeakable delight in such a Prisoner, she who for so long has been a prisoner of Him!

The **eye** is the faith, the fidelity. The Spouse declares that she has just one faith, **one eye**; this faith is pointed in full toward Him, and only to Him[17]. The **hair** and the **eye** represent thus two different modes of *union* with God, by means of love and by faith. She speaks of only **one hair** and only **one eye** because if her love (**hair**) or her faith and fidelity (**eye**) to God were not one, aimed only to God, they would not achieve **wounding** God of love.

And you became wounded by one of my eyes (by my faith): my faith brings me so tightly close to You, my Divine Captive, as to cause You to be **wounded**[1] of love to me, when You saw that I had just one faith (**one eye**) and that my love was just one (**one hair**), only for You, strong as a **neck**.

Symbolic translation:

When You saw that I had detached myself from any other little love, that the whole of my love was only for You, that it was strong, that it was flying toward You propelled by the Holy Spirit without any distractions by anything or by anybody, You gazed at me with love, You became wounded by my love and You became a prisoner of my love.

32

When you at first surmised me
Your gaze was on my eyes imprinted so,
That it effeminized me,
And my eyes were not slow
To worship that which set your own aglow.

Cuando tú me mirabas
tu gracia en mí tus ojos imprimían;
por eso me adamabas
y en eso merecían
los míos adorar lo que en ti vían.

When You looked at me Your eyes imprinted Your grace in me; for this You loved me ardently; and thus my eyes deserved to adore what they beheld in You.

Love captures and binds even God [1]. If you act with love to Him, by love you will bind Him with one **hair** (**hair**: love[2]).

In perfect love you don't take anything for yourself and you don't attribute anything to yourself, but to the beloved. The Spouse here clarifies that what may have looked as attributable to herself in stanza 31 (**capturing the Beloved with one hair** and **wounding Him with**

one eye), was only possible because He had favored her by **looking** at her with love. By means of this **gaze** He made her gracious and pleasing to Himself. From this **grace** that she received from Him, she **deserved** His love, she was granted **to adore** Him in a fashion pleasing to Him, and to perform works worthy of His grace and love.

For God to **look** is for Him to love[3]. When the Spouse says **Your eyes,** she refers to His mercy. He descends in mercy onto her soul and lifts her so high as to make her a partaker of His very divinity [4]. He **loves the** Wayfarer **ardently** because He ardently desires to give him, to **imprint** on him, **grace**, so He could rejoice in him. He gave His Bride love (her **hair**) and faith (her **eye**, formed with his love).

 By **imprinting** His **grace** onto the Bride, God makes her worthy (**deserving**) and capable of His love; His love is **what they beheld in You.** In other words: **because You** have **imprinted Your grace unto me, You loved me ardently**. That is, You gave me more grace on this account. Without His grace one cannot meet His grace, which is to give more grace [5].

God loves nothing outside Himself; He does not love things for what they are in themselves. He loves all things for Himself, within Himself; thus love (**Your grace in me**) becomes the purpose for which He loves (**for this You loved me ardently**). For God, to love the Spouse is to put her somehow in Himself and make her His equal. Thus, He loves the Spouse within Himself, with Himself, in other words, with the very love by which He loves Himself. This is why she **deserves** this love in all of her works insofar as she does them in God. She **adores** Him in every work she does [6]. Lifted to this height, she merits Him in every work.

And thus my eyes deserved means that by the favor and **grace** granted to me by the eyes of Your mercy (**Your eyes**), **when You looked at me** and made me pleasing to Your eyes and worthy of Your sight, **my eyes deserved to adore what they beheld in You**. My faculties (my intellect and my will, which are the **eyes** through which I could see You), were previously in the misery of looking at lowly things; the power to look at God is the power to do works in the grace of God. My faculties (**eyes**) merited (**deserved**) because they **adored** in the grace of God (**what they beheld in You**), by which every work becomes meritorious. They **adored what they** now **saw in You**, which they did not see previously because of their blindness and lowliness. They now **beheld** goodness, love, mercy, and the countless benefits received from You. Previously they did not **deserve to adore** or to **behold** any of this; they did not even deserve to reflect on some of these things about God. Great is the rudeness and the blindness of the Wayfarer without God's grace! He is not even aware of the possibility of looking at Him!

Symbolic Translation:

When You looked at me with love, Your mercy granted me grace upon grace; when You then saw how Your grace and Your love had lifted me, You loved me ardently and You gave me the necessary merit to adore the love that I saw in You.

33

Scorn not my humble ways,
And if my hue is tawny do not loathe me.
On me you may well gaze
Since, after that, the rays
Of every grace and loveliness will clothe me.

No quieras despreciarme
que, si color moreno en mi hallaste,
ya bien puedes mirarme
despues que me miraste,
que gracia y hermosura en mi dejaste.

Do not despise me; for, if You found me dark before, now truly You can look at me since You have looked and left me in grace and beauty.[1,2]

The Bride says **do not despise me**, not out of a desire to be held in high regard for her merits, but because she sees the gifts and grace that God has given her.

For, if you found me dark before: she realizes that her misery, the **dark** color of her soul, comes from herself and she only deserves to be **despised**; she knows that before the Beloved **looked at her**

graciously, He found lowness and the unsightliness of her sins and imperfections. She is aware that her previous sins and every action of hers has permanent consequences[3] and that the only reason for her to have been **looked at** and exalted is in God.

Since You have looked and left me in grace and beauty: the Bride has noted that the gaze of the Beloved has **left her clothed** in His own **beauty**, has lifted her and has given her tokens and richness that she did not have before. God gives her **grace** upon grace[4] for He dwells within her, well pleased with her, and He ordains His **grace** so that the Bride receives more honor and glory; she becomes thus a bright light that on its own account absorbs countless less luminous lights. She is aware that she has been lifted from her former state to such dignity, close to the Bridegroom, and she rejoices with love and gratitude.

Now truly you can look at me: after becoming free from sins and imperfections, she is aware that she deserves, on her own account, for the Beloved to **look at her** often, something she did not deserve before, and she humbly requests continuation of this spiritual union. *Worthy of such honor is the one whom the King honors!*[5] He looks at her time and again, giving her grace after grace[4], until He espouses her to Himself in *spiritual marriage,* and brings her to the inner chamber of His love[6].

The Spouse ponders: the first **look** rubbed off my **dark** color and made me worthy to be seen, because You **looked at me** with love and You clothed me in Your **beauty**. Now, You can **look at me** again and, by receiving more graces from Your eyes, my **grace, beauty** and my merits to be **looked at**, will increase further.

As the Beloved continues to honor and exalt His Spouse, He becomes progressively more captivated and enamored of her[7]; God gives more to whomever has more and His gifts are multiplied in proportion to those possessed by the Wayfarer[8].

Symbolic Translation:

Do not despise me on account of my former sins and imperfections. See how Your loving gaze has lifted me and has left me clothed with graces and beauty; now that You are pleased with me, I beg You to keep looking at me in continuing union with me.

34

The Bridegroom speaks:

> The dove so snowy-white,
> Returning to the Ark, her frond bestows;
> And seeking to unite
> The mate of her delight
> Has found him where the shady river flows.

> *La blanca palomica*
> *al arca con el ramo ha retornado*
> *y ya la tortolica*
> *al socio deseado*
> *en las riberas verdes ha hallado.*

The small white dove has returned to the ark with an (olive) branch; and now the turtledove has found its longed-for mate by the green river banks.[1]

In the previous stanza the Spouse belittled herself, calling herself **dark** and ugly. God customarily exalts those who humble themselves[2] and now He exalts her by calling her **white dove** and describes her purity and her riches for laboring and for preparing herself to come to Him. He also speaks of her bliss in having found the Bridegroom in this union (**now the turtledove has found its longed-for mate**), of the fulfillment of her desires and of the delight and refreshment she possesses in Him, now that the trials of life are over. He is the **green river banks.** He calls her **white** because of the purity imparted by the grace she has found in God; she calls her **dove** [3], who has bright and loving eyes, to denote the loving contemplation by which she looks at God[4] with simplicity and meekness.

The dove at Noah's Ark flew back and forth without finding a place to alight until it returned with an olive branch as a sign of God's mercy and of cessation of the flooding [5]. Similarly, this **dove** left God's **ark** when He created her in her mother's womb[6]; she then passed through the waters of sin and imperfections; she found no place for her appetites to rest [7], and flew to the **ark** to (the Creator's breast) back and forth. He did not take her in until He made all of her sins to cease (the waters of the Flooding), and then she **returned** as **white** as when her soul was created. She carried an olive **branch**, which symbolizes the reward for her merits and her victory over herself and over all things through the mercy of God.

He then calls her **turtledove** because it used to be said that *the turtledove would not perch on a green branch, drink cool clear water, rest in the shade or join the company of others until she finds her mate.*

The Bride has to acquire all these traits of the turtledove in order to **find its longed-for mate,** to reach her union with the Son of God. She advances with such love and solicitude that, like the turtledove, she will not get distracted with any delight (*green branch*), worldly honor or glory (*clear water*), body comfort (*cold water*), favor or protection of anybody (*resting in the shade*), have the *company of other* affections, but sigh for solitude in all things until she *finds her mate,* her Bridegroom.

Finally, the Bride alights on the *green branch* (**by the green river banks**), delighting in her Beloved; she drinks the *clear water* of sublime contemplation; she *rests in the shade* of His protection, where she is divinely and delightfully consoled, nourished and refreshed [1]. The gifts of friendship and expressions of love exchanged between the Bridegroom and the Bride are ineffable [4].

Symbolic Translation:

The Wayfarer has worked hard, without any rest or distraction, and has conquered sin and imperfections; his appetites have ceased and he has become pure. He has found his Beloved, has become his Bride and Spouse, and has reached *union* with Him in simple, meek and loving contemplation. Now the trials of life and time are over for her. All of her desires are fulfilled and she delights and refreshes in Him

35

In solitude she bided,
And in the solitude her nest she made.
In solitude he guided
His loved-one through the shade
Whose solitude the wound of love has made.

En soledad vivía,
y en soledad ha puesto ya su nido,
y en soledad la guía
a solas su querido,
también en soledad de amor herido.

She lived in solitude and now in solitude she has built her nest; and in solitude He guides her, He alone, who also bears the wound of love because of her solitude.[1,2]

God reveals that He communicates to the Spouse and unites Himself to her in the solitude of the poverty of spirit and of detachment. He is pleased in seeing that she is established in the peace and quietude of an unchanging good, which is her love to Him alone. This love is now settled in her; she no longer needs other means or masters[3], for He is now her personal direct guide. He praises the **solitude** in which the Spouse had formerly desired to live, stating how it was a means for her to find and rejoice in Him alone, withdrawn from all other affliction, satisfaction, or support. He states that He was enamored of her because of her desire to live apart from all created things, and He took care of her by accepting her in His arms. He asserts not only that **He guides her**, but that He does so alone, **in solitude**, with no other means (angels, humans, forms, figures), for now she possesses true liberty.

She (the turtledove, the Spouse) **lived in solitude**, in poverty of spirit, detached of any creature, emptying her intellect and her will of any other selfish desire and affection. She had suffered trial and anguish while looking for perfection as Wayfarer and Bride, because then she was still imperfect.

And now in solitude has built her nest: **now**, after her union with the Beloved, she has found refreshment and repose (**has built her nest**) **in** this perfect **solitude** in God.

And in solitude He guides her: the Spouse has emptied her will and her intellect of selfish desires and affections and, once she is empty, alone, **in solitude**, God engages her in the invisible and divine[4]. **He guides her**: He lifts her to the love of God.

He alone guides her, directly, personally, without any means or agents, for she has left all and profits by no other than the Word, Who helps her ascend further.

Who also bears the wound of love because of her solitude: He is wounded with love for the Spouse when He sees that she embraces absolute **solitude** for His sake; **wounded of love** for her, He does not wish to leave her alone and **He alone guides her**, drawing her to Him. Had He not found her in spiritual solitude, He would not have wrought her and absorbed her in Himself.

Symbolic Translation:

The Bride used to live in complete detachment and abandonment of everything else; thus she could settle in her Beloved. Now, free from all other possession, affection or desire, in peace, espoused to her Beloved, He guides her directly, personally, without any agents or intermediaries, and He absorbs her in Himself. He is also wounded of love and obliged to care for her because of her total abandonment to Him.

IV.

In the remaining 5 stanzas the focus shifts from the state of spiritual marriage to prayer for the beatific pasture, which is attained in Heaven.

36

The Spouse speaks:

Rejoice, my love, with me
And in your beauty see us both reflected:
By mountain-slope and lea,
Where purest rills run free,
We'll pass into the forest undetected:

*Gocémonos, amado
y vámonos a ver en tu hermosura
al monte y al collado
do mana el agua pura
y entremos más adentro en la espesura.*

Let us rejoice, Beloved, and let us go forth to behold ourselves in Your beauty to the mountain and to the hill, to where the pure water flows, and further, deep into the thicket.[1]

Love is a union between two, who enjoy each other freely; they would rather be alone together than with a third party. Once the Spouse is at the peak of perfection and freedom, she no longer has any activity to engage in, other than surrender to intimate loving, enjoying in the delights of this pasture[2,3]. When love takes its root, it makes the lovers always desire to taste its joys in the inward and outward exercise of love[4,5]. In this stanza the Spouse asks her Beloved for three things proper to love: *to receive love, to become like the Beloved, and to know the Beloved better.*

To receive the joy and savor of love: **Let us rejoice, Beloved**, beyond the sweetness we already possess in the habitual union of our *spiritual marriage*, into the joy that overflows from the actual practice of love by means of internal, affective acts, and exteriorly in works of service, done by both of us united.

To become like the Beloved: **to behold ourselves in Your beauty**: let us be transformed into each other's beauty: *I shall be You* in Your beauty by the beauty I obtain when I become absorbed into Your beauty, and *You will be* me in the beauty that You obtain from seeing me in Your beauty. I will then share as Your adopted son, by participation in Your beauty, what your natural Son shares with You by essence[6].

To the mountain: the higher wisdom of Your essence. **The hill**, the lower wisdom of You, my God, revealed by beholding Your creatures and Your creation[7]. The sight of Your wisdom will transform me into Your wisdom and will make me owner of all earthly and heavenly things[8].

To where the pure water flows: to where God bestows knowledge of wisdom, called **pure water** because it cleanses and removes phantasies and ignorance.

To know deeper the Beloved and more of His secrets: **and further, deep into the thicket.** The Spouse proposes **let us go further**, because doing so is desirable[9]. **The thicket** consists of all of God's secret wisdom and knowledge. It is so deep and immense that no matter how much the

Spouse knows, she can always enter it **further**[7,10]. **Deep into the ticket** means: let us enter into the depth of all Your secrets, including the intellectual and sensible favors and the paradoxical blessing of experiential knowledge obtained by undergoing interior and exterior suffering, agonizing anxiety [11-13] and the agony of death. Suffering is very beneficial to the Spouse, and these pleasant and painful experiences are all necessary preparations to enter the divine wisdom and help the Spouse to enter **further** within God.

Symbolic Translation:

Let us rejoice, Beloved, beyond the delight of our habitual union, in inner acts of affection and in external works done by both of us united into a single being. Let us both be transformed into each other's beauty, which is Your beauty. Let me be cleansed by Your wisdom and with it let us behold Your own essence and the beauty of Your creatures and Your creation. Let us enter deeper into Your secret wisdom and knowledge by You granting me favors and many kinds of sufferings.

37

Then climb to lofty places
Among the caves and boulders of the granite,
Where every track effaces
And, entering, leave no traces,
And reveal the wine of the pomegranate.

Y luego nos iremos
a las subidas cavernas de la piedra,
que estan bien escondidas,
y allí nos entraremos
y el mosto de granadas gustaremos.

And then we will go on to the high caverns in the rock, which are so well concealed; there shall we enter and taste the fresh juice of the pomegranates[1,2].

And then, after having entered further into the wisdom of the sublime mysteries of God. The **caverns** refer to those mysteries. The **caverns** have countless deep recesses, and each mystery branches into multiple collateral mysteries. **The rock** is Christ[3].

The high caverns refer to the high and deep mysteries of God's wisdom related to Christ (**the rock**), to the union of Christ with God, to the union of humans with God, to God's relating to human beings regarding predestination of good people and foreknowledge of bad people, the harmony between divine justice and mercy, and many others[4]. The Spouse calls those mysteries **the caverns**[1]. **Which are so well concealed** points to the fact that the more mysteries are unveiled by holy doctors, saints and scientists, the more abundant and deeper those mysteries reveal themselves to be[5].

There, at those **high caverns which are so well concealed**: at those mysteries that are inextricable and ever less comprehensible for the human mind. **We** refers to the Beloved and the Spouse together, since they are united in *spiritual marriage* and she can act only together with God. **Shall enter** refers to the most sublime and intimate transformation of the soul in God through love, that will happen to the Spouse upon her **entering** into these mysteries. She thanks and loves the Father again in Jesus Christ and she is transformed in the love of God, with unspeakable love and delight.

The savor of this praise is so delicate as to being totally beyond words, yet she speaks, and she says: **and (we shall) taste the fresh juice of the pomegranates**. The **pomegranates** stand for the mysteries of Christ, the judgments of the wisdom of God and the virtues and attributes uncovered in their knowledge. Each little pomegranate grain represents one of these countless secrets. The **juice** from these pomegranates that they will both taste and drink is the fruition and delight of the love of God overflowing as the drink of the Holy Spirit, a single final product (**juice**) of all the infused knowledge of each of His attributes (each grain of the pomegranate). The Beloved **tastes** it, He gives it to the Spouse, she tastes it and offers it to Him, and they both taste it together (**we**).

Symbolic Translation:

And then, after having gained some wisdom and knowledge by the favors and sufferings that God had granted me, my Beloved Christ and I will enter into the high, deep and well concealed mysteries related to God's wisdom, to Christ, and to God's handling of His children. Upon entering into these mysteries I will undergo the most sublime and intimate transformation of my soul into my Beloved through love, and we will taste the delight of the love of God by means of the infused knowledge of countless mysteries of Christ and of God's judgments, virtues, and attributes.

38

Up there, to me you'll show
What my own soul has longed for all the way:
And there, my love, bestow
The secret which you know
And only spoke about the other day.

Alli me mostrarías
aquello que mi alma pretendía
y luego me darías
alli, tú, vida mía,
aquello que me diste el otro día.

There You will show me what my soul has been seeking and then You will give me, You, my life, will give me there, that what You gave me on that other day[1]

The ultimate reason for everything is love. Lovers can only consider themselves satisfied when they feel that they love as much as they are loved, and the Spouse had always been seeking in all of her acts to love Him totally, perfectly. That is **what my soul has been seeking**. When she says that He **will show** it to her, she is indicating that the Beloved will show her in what way He is going to transform her into His love. She already has true union of her will with His will through her transformation in the Holy Spirit, who is given to her to strengthen her love[2]. However, only in the glory of Heaven will she know God as she is known by Him[3] and she will love Him as He loves her.

And then, *on the day of my espousal and on my day of gladness of heart*[4], when loosened from the flesh and within the **high caverns** of Your chamber, being gloriously transformed in You, having **drank with You the juice of the sweet pomegranates, then You will give me, You, my life, will give me there…**

That is the ineffable, the essential glory of the vision of God, that which is often described in the Scriptures but not explained since it is beyond words [5-16]. Since it is ineffable, the Spouse refers to it as **that**.

What you gave me on that other day: on the day of Creation, when You predestined me to it. That day, like today's day and the day when **you will give me**, is the *present day* of Your eternity. On that day You predestined my soul to glory and You gave it to her freely from all eternity, before You created me within my mother's womb[17].

Symbolic Translation:

There You will show me how to love You perfectly, as I have been always seeking, and then, on that day, as I am being transformed in You, my Beloved, You will give me the ineffable, which You, in your eternal *today*, already gave me on the day of Creation, when You predestined me to it.

39

The breathing of the air,
The song of the sweet nightingale,
The grove and its living beauty
In the serene night,
With a flame that is consuming and painless.

El aspirar del aire,
el canto de la dulce filomena,
el soto y su donaire
en la noche serena,
con llama que consume y no da pena.

The breathing of the air, the song of the sweet nightingale, the grove and its living beauty in the serene night, with a flame that will consummate and causes no pain. [1-3]

In contemplation God transmits to the Wayfarer a knowledge in silence and darkness of the intellect, without him understanding how, without any participation of the mind, without any intervention of forms, thoughts, sensory perceptions, images or intellectual functions. It is a *knowing without knowing* [4,5]

In this stanza, the Spouse can't help but to proclaim what had happened[6,] and she talks about the ineffable **what** that she experiences, mentioned in stanza 38. In each verse she mentions here a different aspect of this **what**: *The Holy Spirit; Jubilation; The knowledge of God, of His creatures and of their orderly arrangement; Contemplation of the divine essence; Total transformation in the immense love of God.*

The Holy Spirit is the **air** she breathes in, she returns breathing it out, and she is breathed into. It is the love **breathed** between the Father, the Son and the Spouse; each one of them aspires and expires the Holy Spirit to and from the other two.

The Spouse experiences, thus, an inner transformation in Them through communication and participation, by the merits of the Son[7-10], in an ineffable and incomprehensible way.

Jubilation: the Spouse can now hear the voice of her Beloved calling her as He would call one who is now ready to make the journey to eternal life[11].

Jubilant with God in the union that is being done onto her, being now able to perform very perfect works, she **sings** like a **sweet nightingale** her delightful jubilations[12] in a highly perfect praise in union with Him, by Him, and in Him[13]. Both voices, the one from the Beloved calling her and her own voice, jubilant, are **the sweet song of the nightingale.**

The knowledge of God, of his creatures and of their orderly arrangement: **the grove** is God, Who gives *being* to all creatures, *nurtures* them, and manifests Itself as the Creator. The **grove** has **living beauty**, which is the grace, wisdom, and beauty that every created being has received from God and manifests in its harmonious relationship to other creatures.

Contemplation: **the night** is the *obscure* contemplation in which these things are received; this *obscure* contemplation is void of thoughts and of sensory perceptions. It happens when a Wayfarer sits with the intention to pray, without doing anything, saying anything, or noticing anything to happen.

Contemplation of the divine essence: **serene** refers to the *clear* contemplation that is a beatific vision of God; the soul receives it in addition to the obscure contemplation of the **night**.

Total transformation in the immense love of God: **the flame** is the love of the Holy Spirit. **Will consummate**: will complete, will bring to perfection. The Spouse affirms that the Beloved will give her **consummated** love, which produces an inner transformation of the Spouse into God. This perfect love **causes no pain** or sadness when its intensity fluctuates, as opposed to what used to happen before. Her **consummated** love is so perfectly conformed to the will of God that the Spouse has **no pain** when she remembers that there is a greater love waiting for her in the beatific life in Heaven.

O souls, created for these grandeurs and called to them! What are you doing? How are you spending your time?

Symbolic translation:

What You will give me is the Holy Spirit, which is love aspired and expired between You, me, and the Father; You will give me to hear Your voice calling me and to hear the jubilation of my response; You will give to me God, Mother of all creatures; You will give me the harmony, grace, and beauty of all of them. You will give that to me in the clear and serene beatific contemplation and in the obscure contemplation void of thoughts, of images and of awareness of being in contemplation. You will give it to me with the love of the Holy Spirit, perfectly transforming me into Him, with conformity to the fluctuating peaks and troughs of such love.

40

With none our peace offending,
Aminadab has vanished with his slaughters:
And now the siege had ending,
The cavalcades descending
Were seen within the precinct of the waters.

Que nadie lo miraba,
Aminadab tampoco parecía
y el cerco sosegaba
y la caballería
a vista de las aguas descendía.

For no one looked at it, nor did Aminadab come close; the siege was still; and the cavalry, at the sight of the waters, descended.[1,2]

The Spouse is aware that she is detached from all earthly or heavenly creatures, indifferent to like or dislike, to pleasure or pain, united to God in utmost delight and in most intimate love, transformed and enriched with abundant graces. She sees herself ready to climb, overflowing in delights, across the dessert of death, to take her glorious seat next to her Beloved [3]. In this stanza she sets out the facts before Him, one in each verse, for Him to be pleased to transfer her from the *spiritual marriage* on earth to the *glorious marriage* in Heaven.

For: so detached of any creature, so indifferent, so recollected with the Beloved.

No one: no creature. **Looked**: reached with their eyes. **At it**: at the intimate delight with the Beloved. **For no one looked at it**: so detached of any creature that none reached her with their gaze or managed to move her out of the deep recollection that she enjoys with the Beloved.

Aminadab[1]: the Devil, who continually tries to prevent her from entering into recollection with the Beloved. **Nor did Aminadab come close**: The Devil did not dare either to come close, because she has conquered temptation and is in the state of perfection.

The siege: passions and appetites all around the Spouse that attract, call, combat, and imprison her. **Was still**: the passions and appetites do not disturb her anymore. **The siege was still**: the passions and appetites do not surround, combat, or imprison her anymore. The passions are now ordained toward God, and the appetites are mortified, annihilated.

The cavalry are the five senses and the phantasy [4]. **The waters** are the spiritual goods that the Spouse drinks, in interior delight with God in this state of *spiritual marriage*[5]. **Descended**: The senses stop perceiving the external stimuli and the mind descends into recollection, into complete silence, facilitating the soul to drink of those **waters**.[6]

At the sight: The spiritual goods are communicated directly to the soul without the senses being able to perceive them. The mind, however, may receive a certain delight (**the sight**). This certain delight, this **sight**, invites to recollection, to silencing the senses. **The cavalry** (the senses), therefore, did not descend *to drink* the waters, but it **descended** *at the sight* of the waters.

The Spouse sets all these circumstances before her Beloved, the Son of God, with the desire for Him to transfer her from the *spiritual marriage* that she enjoys in this Church Militant to the *glorious marriage* in the Church Triumphant in Heaven. May the most sweet Jesus bring there all those who invoke His name. To Him all honour and glory in conjunction with the Father and the Holy Spirit, *in saecula saeculorum. Amen.*

Symbolic translation:

Detached of everything, no creature can turn my attention away from my profound recollection in the Beloved. The Devil approaches me no more to tempt me, since he sees that I have reached the state of perfection. The passions and appetites no longer disturb me; the former are ordained toward God, the latter, mortified. The senses become quiet and the mind descends into complete silence, glancing the delights and spiritual goods of the *glorious marriage* with the Beloved in Heaven.

Notes

Introduction (1)- F. Brändle, OCD: *Biblia en San Juan de la Cruz*, Editorial de Espiritualidad, Madrid 1990, ISBN 84.7068.206.7 page 26 **(2)-** St. John of the Cross. *Spiritual Canticle*, Introduction, paragraph 2. In *Collected Works*, ICS Publications, Washington DC 1991; from now on, referred to as **John, Works (3)-** St. Teresa of Jesus *Interior Castle*, Fourth Mansions, chapter 3 paragraph 4. In *Complete Works*, Volume 2, Sheed and Ward, London 1946. From now on, referred to as **Teresa, Works (4)-** The Jerusalem Bible, Dalton Longman Todd, London 1974, ISBN 0-232-51283-3. **(5)-** The Holy Bible Douay Version, translated to English from the Latin Vulgate, Douay, AD 1609: Rheims, AD 1582, London, Catholic True Society 1957. **(6)-** Biblia Sacra Vvlgatae, Editionis Romae, ex Typographia Apostolica Vaticana, 1592 (Library, Abadía Benedictina de Santo Domingo de Silos; Biblia Vulgata in Latin) **(7)-** Comment to the word *Jehova*. Diccionario Enciclopédico de la Biblia, Centro: Informática y Biblia Abadía de Maredsous, Bélgica, Dirección: Longton y Poswick. Spanish edition by Miquel Gallart, Herder Publisher, Barcelona 1993.**(8)-** Dictionaire de la Bible, Tome Troisiéme, Publie par F. Vigoroux. Editeurs Letouzey et Anè, Paris, 1903, page 1219- 1244 **(9)-** Numerous personal communications, e.g. by the Bishop of Whales, by a monk of the Benedictine Abbey of St Domingo de Silos, etc. **(10)-** Swami Prabhavananda, C. Isherwood: *Shankara's Crest jewel of discrimination*, Vedanta Press 1975, Hollywood, CA, USA **(11)-** John, *Works*. Poem Living Flame of Love.

(12)- I. Matthews: The impact of God. Hodder & Stoughton, London 1995, ISBN 10:0.340.61257.6, p. 54- 56

Stanza 1 (1)- *My Beloved is like a gazelle, like a young stag…On my bed, at night, I sought him whom my heart loves. I sought him but did not find him. So I will rise and go through the City; in the streets and the squares I will seek him whom my heart loves; I sought him but did not find him…I opened to my Beloved, but he had turned his back and gone! My soul failed at his flight. I sought him but did not find him. I called him but he did not answer.* Sg 2.9 and 3.1-2 and 5.6 **(2)-** The Buddha says: *sabbe sankhara anicca: all is transient.* Dhammapada, translated by Juan Mascaró, Penguin Classics, London 1973, verse 277, p 75 **(3)-** *Tell me then, you whom my heart loves: where will you take your flock to graze, where will you rest it at noon?* Sg 1.7 **(4)-** *He made darkness his covering, the dark waters of the clouds, his tent.* Ps. 17:12 **(5)-** *We need to make ourselves indifferent to all created things…we should not want health more than illness, wealth more than poverty…* St. Ignatius of Loyola, Spiritual Exercises, Anthony Clarke Books, Wheathampstead 1963, SBN 85.650.033, Paragraph 23, p 22, Principle and Foundation. **(6)-** *Find a place where we can be alone and look upon him present within us… The soul collects together all the faculties and enters within itself to be with its God…those who are able to shut themselves up in this way…and who have formed the habit of looking at nothing and staying in no place which will distract these outward senses…it withdraws the senses from all outward things and spurns them so completely that, without its understanding how, its eyes close…turn your eyes upon yourself and look at yourself inwardly…this is not a supernatural state but depends upon our volition…we can enter it of our own accord…this is not a silence of the faculties: it is a shutting-up of the faculties within itself by the soul…we must recollect our outward senses, take charge of them ourselves and give them something which will occupy them...* Teresa, *Works*, Way of Perfection chapters 28- 29 pp 114 – 122. **(7)-** *Pratyahara ("pulling towards itself") is the withdrawal of the senses from their contact with their objects, inward, towards their source, the mind.* PV

Karambelkar. Patañjala Yoga Sutras, Kaivalyadhama, Lonavla, India, 1987, Sutra 2: 54 pp 335. **(8)-** Brother Lawrence: The Practice of the Presence of God, Wilder Publications, Radford VA, USA, 2008 **(9)-** The same idea is expressed by a XIIIth century Sufi mystic: *He is concealed of you because of you, and you are concealed from you because of you. So separate from you, and you shall witness Him.* Shaik Wali Raslan Ad- Dimashqi: *Risala fi't- Tawhid* (Concerning the Affirmation of Divine Oneness), translated by Muhtar Holland, Al-Baz Publishing Inc, Hollywood, Florida, USA, AD 1997, ISBN1-882216-05-9, page 9. From now on, referred to as **Risala**. **(10)-** *Indeed you are a hidden God.* Is. 45:15 **(11)-** See note Introduction, 12 (Matthews) page 82- 83, 132.

Stanza 2 (1)- *Tell me then, you whom my heart loves: where will you lead your flock to graze, where will you rest it at noon? That I may no more wander like a vagabond beside the flock of your companions…Feed me with raisin cakes, restore me with apples, for I am sick with love…I charge you, daughters of Jerusalem, if you should find my Beloved, what must you tell him? That I am sick with love.* Sg 1.7 and 2.5 and 5.8 **(2)-** *Yahweh is my shepherd, I lack nothing. In meadows of green he lets me lie. To the waters of repose he leads me; there he revives my soul.* Ps. 22:2 **(3)-** *Gabriel- it is he who has brought the Qur'an down upon your heart, by permission of Allah.* The Qur'an, Surat 2:97 Al Baqarah (the cow). **(4)-***…the angel of the Lord appeared to him in a dream and said, "Joseph, son of David, do not be afraid to take Mary…"* Mt. 1:20. **(5)-** *In the sixth month the angel Gabriel was sent by God to a town in Galilee called Nazareth, to a virgin betrothed to a man named Joseph, of the house of David…* Lk. 1:26-27 **(6)-** *See that you never despise any of these little ones, for I tell you that their angels in heaven are continually in the presence of my Father in heaven.* Mt. 18:10 **(7)-** *You must love the Lord your God with all your heart, with all your soul, with all your strength, and with all your mind, and your neighbour as yourself.* Lk. 10:27. **(8)-** The posture of the Buddha, *mudra abhaya*, that symbolizes *freedom from fear*, is sitting in the lotus posture, with a hand raised. N. Tingley: Buddhas,

Pomegranate Publication, Petaluma, California, USA, 2009. **(9)-** *Be not afraid*. John Paul II: apostolic letter to those responsible for communications, 24 January 2005. **(10)-** *In love there can be no fear, but fear is driven out by perfect love; because to fear is to expect punishment, and anyone who is afraid is still imperfect in love.* 1 Jn. 4:18. **(11)-** *Sacrifice*: to make something holy, to cause something to become holy. From Latin *facere*: to make, to cause something to become, and *sacrum, sacred. Longman Dictionary of the English Language*, Essex, United Kingdom 1988, ISBN 0-582-555-116 **(12)-** Saññyasi (Sanskrit: the one who lays all down, i.e. the one who renounces to all, i.e. the ascet) is the one who acts only as a sacrifice: *He who performs all obligatory action without depending on the fruit thereof, is a saññasin and a yogi*. The Bhagavad Gita according to Gandhi, Wilder Publications, Blacksburg, VA, 2011, discourse VI verse 1, p 48. *Whatever you do, whatever you eat, whatever you offer or give away, and whatever austerities you perform, do that as an offering to Me.* Ibid, Discourse IX verse 27. **(13)-** John 2:3

Stanza 3 (1)- *The watchmen came upon me on their rounds in the City: "Have you seen him whom my heart loves?" Scarcely I had passed them than I found him whom my heart loves… The watchmen came upon me as they made their rounds in the City. They beat me, they wounded me, they took away my cloak, they who guard the ramparts.* Sg 3. 3-4 and 5.7. **(2)-** *Search and you will find* Mt. 7:7.**(3)-** *It is not those who say to me "Lord, Lord" who will enter the Kingdom of Heaven, but the person who does the will of my Father in heaven.* Mt. 7:21. **(4)-** H. Thurston, S.J. The physical phenomena of mysticism. Burns Oats, London 1952 **(5)-** *They are obstacles in the path to union, but miraculous powers in the life of worldliness.* P.V. Karambelkar. Patañjala Yoga Sutras, Kaivalyadhama, Lonavla, India, 1987. Sutra 3.37 p 446. **(6)-** see note 1:2 **(7)-** see note 1.5 **(8)-** For the training and practice of indifference see www.sjweb.info and www.dhamma.org **(9)-** *Love is experienced only after certainty, and when the lover is sincere in his love, his heart must be empty of* *all that is apart from Him. And as long as it retains any trace of love for anything but Him, he must be lacking in love.* See note 1.9 Risala. **(10)-** Torquato Torío de la Riva: Catecismo de los padres Ripalda y Astete, second edition, volume I, Madrid 1820, Ibarra press, page 31 **(11)** *Then Jesus was led by the Spirit out into the wilderness to be tempted by the devil.* Mt. 4:1. **(12)-** *You must not love this passing world or anything that is in the world. The love of the Father cannot be in any man who loves the world, because nothing the world has to offer- the sensual body, the lustful eye, pride in possessions- could ever come from the Father, but only from the world.* 1 Jn. 2:15-16. **(13)-** *Since self-indulgence is the opposite of the Spirit; the Spirit is totally against such a thing.* Gal. 5:17. **(14)-** *The Law, of course, as we all know, is spiritual; but I am unspiritual; I have been sold as a slave to sin. The fact is, I know of nothing good living in me- living, that is, in my unspiritual self- for though the will to do what is good is in me, the performance is not.* Rom. 7:14, 18.

Stanza 4 (1)- *The watchmen came upon me on their rounds in the City: "Have you seen him whom my heart loves?"* Sg 3.3. **(2)-** See note 2.2

Stanza 5: None

Stanza 6 (1)- *You made us for yourself, O Lord, and our heart is restless until it rests in you.* St Augustine, Confessions, Book 1, Chapter 1, paragraph 1. **(2)-** A Sanskrit aphorism says: *vidya avidyahá; avidya vidyahá: knowledge (of what is not God) (is) ignorance (of God); ignorance (of what is not God) (is) knowledge (of God).* Id est: the various knowledges make it difficult for us to perceive God directly. Direct perception of God shows knowledge of anything else to be confusion, ignorance. **(3)-** *I bless you, Father, Lord of heaven and of earth, for hiding these things from the learned and the clever and revealing them to mere children.* Mt. 11:25.

Stanza 7 (1)- Wandering, from Latin *vacant*, free. Those who wander, who are free, who walk in freedom. **(2)-** One of the graces that God grants in this world to selected persons is the so called *prayer of union*, which characterizes the Fifth Dwelling Place of St. Teresa of Jesus, where there is an experience of God with no duality, with no distinction between *me* and *not-me* (in that sense, like in dreamless sleep). At its end, the soul knows with absolute certainty that she has visited God and been visited by Him; she has perfect consciousness of what she has experienced, and comes out of that prayer transformed, with an intense desire to serve God. Sister Mary of St. Joseph, OCD: personal communication. **(3)-** *For the short time that the condition lasts, the soul has no consciousness and has no power to think…*(chapter 1 p 248). *For as long as a soul is in this state, it can neither see nor hear nor understand…God implants Himself in the interior of that soul in such a way that, when it returns to itself, it cannot possibly doubt that God has been in it and it has been in God; so firmly does this truth remain within it that, although for years God may never grant it that favour again, it can neither forget nor doubt that it has received it* (p 251)*…the silkworms feed on the mulberry-leaves until they are full grown…with their mouths they start spinning silk, making themselves very tight little cocoons, in which they bury themselves. Then, finally, the worm, which was quite large and ugly, comes right out of the cocoon as a beautiful white butterfly* (chapter 2 p 253). St. Teresa, *Works*, Interior Castle, Fifth Mansions. **(4)-** *Samadhi (*a contemplative state of integration, of union, where there is no duality*), though devoid of anything which may be called an experience in the usual sense, changes the personality of the individual in a most marked manner.* (p 24, commentary to Sutra 1.10). *In this transcendence, I- am-ness is also lost…whatever happens further cannot be called experience in the strict or usual sense. There is no "I" and therefore there is no experiencer, at least in the sense that an experience should be describable…*(p 51, commentary to Sutra 1.17). P.V. Karambelkar. Patañjala Yoga Sutras, Kaivalyadhama, Lonavla, India, 1987. **(5)-** Gen. 30:1 **(6)-** *At night I open the window and ask the moon to come and press her face against mine. "Breathe into me…breathe into me; close the language door and open the window of love". The moon won't use the door; only the window.*

Jalal-ad-din Rumi, in: Coleman B: The soul of Rumi, Harper Collins, New York 2001; ISBN 10-00-6060-4522

Stanza 8 (1)- *It is in Him that we live, and move and exist.* Acts 17:28.

Stanza 9 (1)- These expressions describe the painful void caused by the *passive night of the spirit.* John, *Works,* Dark Night of the Soul II.6.5, page 405. **(2)-** See note 2.12

Stanza 10 (1)- *...yes, with you is the fountain of life, by your light we see the light.* Ps. 35:10 **(2)-** *...the light of my eyes itself has left me.* Ps. 37:11. **(3)-** *Can I ever be happy again? I am a blind man; I no longer see the light of heaven; I am sunk in darkness like the dead who see the light no more.* Tob 5:12 **(4)-** *The heavenly city has no need of the sun or the moon to shine in it, because the brightness of God illumines it, and the Lamb is the lamp thereof.* Rev. 21:23.

Stanza 11 (1)- *My dove, hiding in the clefts of the rock, in the coverts of the cliff, show me your face, let me hear your voice; for your voice is sweet and your face is beautiful.* Sg 2:14 **(2)-** Keating T: Open mind, open heart. Ed Continuum International Publishing Group, New York 2006, ISBN 987-0-8264-1889-0 page 40 **(3)-** Laird M: into the silent land. Oxford University Press, Oxford, United Kingdom 2006 ISBN 13: 978-0-19-530.760-3, page. 16- 17 **(4)-** *...no human shall see me and live.* Ex. 33:20

Stanza 12 (1)- *Within each soul there is a mansion for God... when His Majesty is pleased to grant the soul... this Divine Marriage, He... brings it into His own Mansion...the Lord unites it with himself...but He makes it blind and dumb...and so prevents it from having any sense of how or in what way that favour comes, which is the realization of its nearness to God...by means of an intellectual vision (a certainty with no visual images)... the Most Holy Trinity reveals itself, in all three Persons...although nothing is seen by the eyes, either by the body or of the* *soul... she feels that They have never left her...in all that belongs to the service of God she is more alert than before; and when not otherwise occupied, she rests in that happy companionship.....the soul is always aware that it is experiencing this companionship...however numerous were her trials and business worries, the essential part of her soul seemed never to move from that dwelling-place. So in a sense she felt that her soul was divided; and when she was going through great trials, shortly after God had granted her this favour, she complained of that division, just as Martha complained of Mary (Lk. 10:40)... So subtle is the division perceptible between them that sometimes the operation of the one seems as different from that of the other as are the respective joys that the Lord is pleased to give them... This secret union takes place in the deepest center of the soul, which must be where God Himself dwells....the spirit of the soul is made one with God...He has been pleased to unite Himself with His creature in such a way that they have become like the two who cannot be separated from one another...The* Spiritual Betrothal *is different: here the two persons are frequently separated...in this other favour (*Spiritual Marriage*) it is not so: the soul remains all the time in that center with its God. We might say that* union *is as if the ends of two wax candles were joined so that the light they give is one... the wax and the light are all one; yet afterwards the one candle can be perfectly separated from the other and the candles become two again... But here it is like rain falling from the heavens into a river or a spring; there is nothing but water there and it is impossible to divide or separate the water belonging to the river from that which fell from the heavens. Or it is as if a tiny streamlet enters the sea, from which it will find no way of separating itself, or as if in a room there were two large windows through which the light streamed in: it enters in different places but it all becomes one....His Majesty went on to say...I am in them (Jn. 17:23)...in this state the soul can actually see their truth for itself...when it finds itself in this state...it refrains more carefully from committing the smallest offence against God. It is also strongly desirous of serving Him...the passions are already vanquished...the little butterfly has now died, full of joy at having found rest, and within her lives Christ...there is a self-forgetfulness which is so complete that it really seems as though the soul no longer existed...so entirely is she employed in seeking the honour of*

God...they bear no enmity to those who ill-treat them...they conceive a special love for them...these souls have a marked detachment from everything...all the favours which the Lord grants the soul here come quite independently of the acts of the soul...the soul has seen so much in this Mansion that it can be frightened at nothing...they have no lack of crosses, but these don't unsettle them or deprive them of their peace...the Presence of the Lord which they have within them makes them forget everything...the Lord does not look so much at the magnitude of anything we do as at the love with which we do it. Teresa, *Works*, Interior Castle, Seventh Mansions, Chapters 1- 4 pp 331- 350. **(2)-** *But anyone who drinks the water I shall give will never be thirsty again: the water I shall give will turn into a spring inside him, welling up to eternal life.* Jn. 4:14. **(3)-** *If any man is thirsty, let him come to me! Let the man come and drink who believes in me. He was speaking of the Spirit which those who believed in him were to receive.* Jn. 7:37, 39. **(4)-** *And I live now not with my own life, but with the life of Christ who lives in me.* Gal. 2:20.

Stanza 13 (1)- *Turn away thy eyes from me, for they have made me flee away.* Sg 6.4. **(2)-** *These violent raptures occur at the* betrothal stage, *also called stage of the* Proficients. *The spirit is taken off the body and perceptions stop, for example the perception of pain. God reveals himself and he places virtues and gifts on the soul. A strong communication occurs, with overflowing of God, with a glimpse of what he is. Later, at the stage of* spiritual marriage, *or stage of* Perfects, *all communications are received in peace, with gentle love, and the raptures cease, which are just communications that prepare the soul to receive the* spiritual marriage. John, *Works*, The Spiritual Canticle stanza 13 p 522. **(3)-** *If I have all the eloquence of men or of angels, but speak without love, I am simply a gong booming or a cymbal clashing. If I have the gift of prophecy, understanding all the mysteries there are, and knowing everything, and if I have faith in all its fullness, to move mountains, but without love, then I am nothing at all. If I give away all that I possess, piece by piece, and if I even let them take my body to burn it, but I am without love, it will do me no good whatever.* 1 Cor. 13:1- 3. **(4)-** *Love is always* patient and kind; it is never jealous; love is never boastful or conceited; it is never rude or selfish; it does not take offence, and is not resentful. Love takes no pleasure in other people's sins but delights in the truth; it is always ready to excuse, to trust, to hope, and to endure whatever comes. 1 Cor. 13:4-7.

Stanzas 14- 15 (1)- *My Beloved is fresh and ruddy, to be known among ten thousand. His head is golden, purest gold, his locks are palm fronds and black as the raven. His eyes are doves at a pool of water, bathed in milk, at rest on a pool. His cheeks are beds of spices, banks sweetly scented. His lips are lilies, distilling pure myrrh. His hands are golden, rounded, set with jewels of Tarshish. His belly a block of ivory covered with sapphires. His legs are alabaster columns set in sockets of pure gold. His appearance is that of Lebanon, unrivalled as the cedars. His conversation is sweetness itself, he is altogether lovable. Such is my Beloved, such is my friend, O daughters of Jerusalem.* Sg 5.10-16 **(2)-** *Veil after veil is lifted, veil after veil is behind* (fragment of a poem) V. Bangar, personal communication. **(3)-** *I heard a sound coming out of the sky like the sound of the ocean or the roar of thunder; it seemed to be the sound of harpists playing their harps.* Rev. 14:2. **(4)-** *When Pentecost day came round, they had all met in one room, when suddenly they heard what sounded like a powerful wind from heaven, the noise of which filled the entire house…* Acts 2:1-2. **(5)-** *Father, glorify your name! A voice came from heaven,* I have glorified it, and I will glorify it again!. *People standing by, who heard this, said it was a clap of thunder…* Jn. 12:28-29. **(6)-***After the earthquake came a fire. But Yahweh was not in the fire. And after the fire there came the sound of a gentle breeze. And when Elijah heard this, he covered his face with his cloak and went out and stood at the entrance of the cave. Then a voice came to him.* 1 Kings 19:12-13. **(7)-** See Introduction, note 12 (Matthews page 52- 57). **(8)** –In Hinduism, the apparent universe is Maya, illusion; only Brahman is the absolute ultimate reality. The philosopher and mystic Sankara compares the new perception of the reality, following mystical awakening, with the discovery that, what we took as a snake at the half-light of sensory knowledge, when looked at the light of the supernatural knowledge, we see that it is not a snake but just a rope. See Introduction, note 10 (Sankara). **(9)** – See stanza 35 *She lived in solitude*

Stanza 16 (1)- *Catch the foxes for us, the little foxes that make havoc of the vineyards, for our vineyards are in flower.* Sg 2:15. **(2)-** *...Forgetting all, my quest / ended, I stayed lost to myself at last. / All ceased: my face was pressed / upon my Love, at rest, / with all my cares among the lilies cast. (Literal translation:* **I stayed and forgot myself, laying my face on my Beloved; all things ceased; I abandoned myself, leaving my cares forgotten among the lilies.***)* John, *Works*, poem *The dark night.*

Stanza 17 (1)- *Arise, O north wind, and come, O south wind: blow through my garden, and let the aromatical spices thereof flow...My beloved is gone down into his garden to the bed of aromatical spices, to feed in the gardens and to gather lilies. I to my beloved, and my beloved to me, who feedeth among the lilies.* Sg 4.16 and 6.2-3. **(2)-***...as he came down from the mountain, Moses had the two tablets of the Testimony in his hands- he did not know that the skin of his face was radiant after speaking with Yahweh. And when Aaron and all the sons of Israel saw Moses, the skin of his face shone so much that they would not venture near him.* Ex. 34:29-30. **(3)-***...was accompanied by such a brightness that the Israelites could not bear looking at the face of Moses, though it was a brightness that faded, then how much greater will be the brightness that surrounds the administering of the Spirit!* 2 Cor. 3:7-8.

Stanza 18 (1)- *I charge you, daughters of Jerusalem, by the gazelles, by the hinds of the field, not to stir my love, nor rouse it, until it please to awake.* Sg 2.7 and 8.4. **(2)-** The same idea is found in the Yoga system: *Yogaschittavrittinirodhá* (Yoga {*mystical union*} *is bringing to complete cessation the functional modifications of* chitta {*the mind*}). See P.V. Karambelkar: Patañjala Yoga Sutras, Kaivalyadhama, Lonavla, India, 1987, page 5, Sutra 1:2. **(3)-**The Song of Songs uses the wording *daughters of Jerusalem* in various places, for example in 2.7 and elsewhere. St. John of the Cross replaces it here with *nymphs of Judea.* The metric of his poem would be kept with *daughters of Judea.* Perhaps he tried thus to stress the component of *active, insisting attraction* of the affects, appetites and mental images which thus disturb the intention of remaining in *the most profound center* of the soul. The most profound center of the soul is the see of the Seventh Mansion of St. Teresa of Jesus, where the *Transforming Union* takes place. St. John of the Cross (Works) refers to it in his poem Living Flame: *O Living flame of love / that, burning, dost assail / my inmost soul with tenderness untold, / since thou dost freely move, / deign to consume the veil / which sunders this sweet converse that we hold...* (Literal translation: **O living flame of love that tenderly wounds my soul in its deepest center! Since now you are not oppressive, now consummate! if it be your will: tear through the veil of this sweet encounter!..).**

Stanza 19 (1)- *Love* is for the most part a manifestation of the will; it is the free gift of the person to the beloved. For this reason the Wayfarer asks God to illuminate his will by giving him love. The feeling associated with love is mentioned in stanza 25. See also the comment on love at the second to the last paragraph of the introduction. **(2)-** *He who is endowed with direct experience has neither might nor strength, neither choice nor will, neither movement nor rest.* See note 1.9 Risala, page 8. **(3)-** See stanzas 2, 5- 7, 10, 11 **(4)-** See stanzas 32- 33 **(5)-** *Jesus looked steadily at him and loved him, and he said, "There is one thing you lack. Go and sell everything you own and give the money to the poor"...* Mc. 10:21.

Stanzas 20- 21 (1)- See note 18.1 **(2)-** *Save me, my God, for the waters have come in even unto my soul.* Ps. 68:2. **(3)-** *I opened the mouth of my hope and drew- in the breath of my desires because I longed and hoped for your commandments.* Ps. 118:131. **(4)-** *My heart grew hot within me, and in my meditation a fire shall* *be enkindled.* Ps. 38:4. **(5)**- *She is a garden enclosed, my sister, my promised bride.* Sg 4:12. **(6)**- *I conjure you, daughters of Jerusalem, by the gazelles, by the hinds of the field, not to stir my love, nor rouse it, until it please to awake.* Sg 3:5. **(7)**- *...My soul is disentangled / from every created thing / and lifted above itself / In a life of gladness / supported only in God. / So now it can be said / that I most value this: / My soul now sees itself / without support yet with support.* John, *Works*, poem: A Gloss, with spiritual meaning. **(8)**- *Who is this arising like the dawn, fair as the moon, resplendent as the sun, terrible as an army with banners?* Sg 6:10. **(9)**- Ph. 4:7. **(10)**- Jn. 4:10, 14 **(11)**- Mt. 6:10 **(12)** -Lk. 22:41

Stanza 22 (1)- *He brought me into the cellar of wine; he set in order charity in me...Thy neck is as the tower of David, which is built with bulwarks: a thousand bucklers hang upon it, all the armour of valiant men...His left hand is under my head, and his right hand shall embrace me.* Sg 2.4 and 4.4 and 2.6. **(2)**- *If anyone is seeking God, the Beloved is seeking that person much more... God sends... his divine inspirations and touches, by which he draws her..., bound by the perfection of his law and of faith. It is by means of this perfection that a person must always draw closer to him... The desire for himself that God grants... is a preparation for other more precious and delicate touches... until the soul is so delicately and purely prepared that it merits union with him and substantial transformation* (into him). John, *Works*, The Living Flame of Love, stanza 3.28 page 684. **(3)**- See note 1.9 (Raslan). **(4)**- *What man among you with a hundred sheep, losing one, would not leave the ninety-nine in the wilderness and go after his missing one till he found it? And when he found it, would he not joyfully take it on his shoulders and then, when he got home, call together his friends and neighbours? "Rejoice with me," he would say, "I have found my sheep that was lost."* Lk. 15:4-5. **(5)**-*...what woman with ten drachmas would not, if she lost one, light a lamp and sweep out the house and search thoroughly till she found it? And then, when she had found it, call together her friends and neighbours? "Rejoice with me," she would say, "I have found the drachma I lost."* Lk. 15:8-9. **(6).** *Go forth, daughters of Zion, and* *behold king Solomon in the crown with which his mother crowned him on the day of his espousal and on the day of the joy in his heart.* Sg. 3.11. **(7)-** *...and he, as a bridegroom coming out of his bride-chamber.* Ps. 18:6. **(8)-** Sg 2: 11- 12. A longer paragraph is what one can think of God saying to you at the time of your death, or at specific times when He wants you to free yourself from attachments: *Arise, make haste, my love, my dove, my beautiful one, and come! For winter is now past, the rain is over and gone. The flowers have appeared in our land; the time of pruning is come; the voice of the turtle is heard in our land; the fig-tree hath put forth her green figs; the vines in flower yield their sweet smell. Arise, my love, my beautiful one, and come.* Sg 2: 11- 13.

Stanza 23 **(1)-** *Who is this that cometh up from the desert, flowing with delights, leaning upon her beloved? Under the apple tree I raised you up; there your mother was corrupted, there she who bore you was violated...As the apple- tree among the trees of the woods, so is my beloved among the sons. I sat down under his shadow, whom I desired; and his fruit was sweet to my palate.* Sg 8.5 and 2.3. **(2)-** *And the woman saw that the tree was good to eat, and fair to the eyes, and delightful to behold; and she took of the fruit thereof, and did eat, and gave to her husband who did eat.* Gen. 3:6.

Stanza 24 (1)- *How beautiful are you, my Beloved, and how delightful! Our bed is flourishing!...the hairs of thy head are as the purple of the king bound in the channels.* Sg. 1:15 and 7. 5 **(2)-** *Thy neck is as the tower of David, which is built with bulwarks: a thousand bucklers hang upon it, all the armour of valiant men.* Sg. 4.4 **(3)-** *The pillars thereof he made of silver, the seat of gold, the going up of purple; the midst he covered with charity for the daughters of Jerusalem.* Sg. 3.10 **(4)-** Sg. 2:1

Stanza 25 (1)- (the Spouse): *if thou know not thyself, O fairest among women, go forth and follow after the steps of the flocks, and feed thy goats beside the tents of the shepherds...* (the Bride) *Thy breasts are better than wine, smelling sweet of the* best ointments. *Thy name is as oil poured out… Draw me; we will run after thee to the odour of thy ointments. The king hath brought me into his storerooms…* Sg 1:7 and 1: 1-3 **(2)-** *Draw me, and we shall run after you in the fragrance of your ointments. We run in the odor of your ointments; the maidens have loved you exceedingly.* Sg 1.3 **(3)-** *I will take hold of thee and bring thee into my mother's house; there thou shall teach me and I will give thee a cup of spiced wine and new juice of my pomegranates.* Sg 8.2 **(4)-** *My Beloved put his hand through the opening, and my belly trembled at his touch.* Sg 5.4 **(5)-** St. Teresa of Jesus calls these **sparks** *Prayer of (Passive) Recollection.* Teresa, *Works*, Interior Castle, Fourth Mansions, Chapter 3 pp240- 244 **(6)-** See note 20.4 (Ps. 38:4) **(7)-** *When you enlarged my heart I run the way of your commandments.* Ps. 118:32.

Stanza 26 (1)- *He put me in the secret wine cellar and set in order charity in me.* Sg 2.4. **(2)-** Teresa, *Works,* The Interior Castle, Seventh Mansions. **(3)-** See reference 6.2 **(4)-** *Because wisdom of this world is foolishness to God…An unspiritual person is one who does not accept anything of the Spirit of God; he sees it all as nonsense; it is beyond his understanding because it can only be understood by means of the Spirit.* 1 Cor. 3:19 and 2:14. **(5)-** see the last 3 sentences from the commentary to stanza 27: *Just as the bee, when she goes from flower to flower only extracts honey from them, and does not use them for anything else, similarly the soul united to God in love, extracts only the sweetness of love from all that happens to her. She loves God in everything; she perceives nothing else in anything. Everything leads her to love and she loves God in everything. She knows nothing but love.*

Stanza 27 (1)- See note 26.1 (Sg. 2.4) **(2)-** *I to my Beloved, and his turning is toward me. Come, my Beloved, let us go into the field…and go to the vineyards to see if the vine is in flower…if the pomegranates flourish; there I will give you my breasts.* Sg. 7. 10- 13. **(3)-** *At the breasts of Yahweh you shall be carried and upon his knees you will be caressed.* Is. 66:12. **(4)-** *Elohim, you are my God; I* *am seeking you, my soul is thirsting for you, my flesh is longing for you, a land parched, weary and waterless.* Ps. 62:2. **(5)-** *Over all these clothes, to keep them together and complete them, put on love.* Col. 3:14. **(6)-** *The kingdom of heaven is like treasure hidden in a field which someone has found; he hides it again, goes off happy, sells everything he owns and buys the field.* Mt. 13:44.

Stanza 28 (1)- See note 26.1 (Sg 2.4) **(2)-** See note 2.12 (Gita) **(3)-** *When I was a child, I used to talk like a child, and think like a child, and argue like a child, but now I am a man, all childish ways are put behind me.* 1 Cor. 13:11. **(4)-** *Our method is love, not labour, and annihilation, not perpetuity. When you enter into work, you belong to you, and when you enter into love, you belong to Him. The worshiper looks to his worship, while the lover looks to his beloved.* See note 1.9 (Risala, page 8)

Stanza 29 (1)- *She had a sister called Mary, who sat down at the Lord's feet and listened to him speaking. Now Martha who was distracted with all the serving said, "Lord, do you not care that my sister is leaving me to do the serving all by myself? Please tell her to help me." But the Lord answered: "Martha, Martha," he said, "you worry and fret about so many things, and yet few are needed, indeed only one. It is Mary who has chosen the better part."* Lk. 10:39-42 **(2)-** *No one can be the slave of two masters: he will either hate the first and love the second, or treat the first with respect and the second with scorn. You cannot be the slave both of God and of Money.* Mt. 6:24.

Stanza 30 (1)- *In the morning we will go to the vineyards. We will see if the vines are budding, if their blossoms are opening, if the pomegranate trees are in flower. Then I shall give you the gift of my love.* Sg. 7.12- 13 **(2)-** *We shall make you golden earrings and beads of silver.* Sg. 1.11. **(3)-** *My virtue is at its best in weakness.* 2 Cor. 12:9. **(4)-** God attracts the soul and she labours in perfecting herself; both work helping one another in a coordinated way, like the oars of a boat. Sister Mary of St. Joseph, OCD, personal communication. **(5)-** *On your right hand stands the queen in a garment of gold* (i.e., fenced with gifts and perfect virtues). Ps. 44:10.

Stanza 31 (1)- *Thou hast wounded my heart, my sister, my spouse, thou hast wounded my heart with one of thy eyes, and with one hair of thy neck.* Sg 4.9 (Vulgate Douay, English). *Vulnerasti cor meum soror mea, sponsa, vulnerasti cor meum in uno oculorum tuorum et in uno crine colli tu).* (Vulgate Latin). *(See Introduction notes 5&6)* **(2)-** Stanza 30 explains why the hair in the Song of Songs and in Stanza 31 is just *one hair.* **(3)-** *Over all these clothes, to keep them together and complete them, put on love.* Col. 3:14. **(4)-** *(The Beloved:) I am the rose of Sharon, the Lily of the valleys.* Sg 2:1. **(5)-** *My bonds are cut, my debts are paid, my door has been opened, I go everywhere. They crouch in their corner and weave their web of pale hours, they count their coins sitting in the dust and call me back. But my sword is forged, my armour is put on, my horse is eager to run. I shall win my kingdom.* Rabindranath Tagore: Fruit gathering. The Macmillan Company, New York, 1916 **(6)-** *After the earthquake came a fire, but Yahweh was not in the fire. And after the fire there came the sound of a gentle breeze. And when Elijah heard this, he covered his face with his cloak and went out and stood...* 1 Kings 19:12-13. **(7)-** See note 19.5. **(8)-** *And the Word was made flesh and he lived among us.* Jn. 1:14. **(9)** - *For the bread of God is that which comes down from heaven...because I have come from heaven, not to do my own will, but to do the will of the one who sent me...I am the living bread which has come down from heaven...what if you should see the Son of man ascend to where he was before?* Jn. 6:33, 38, 51, 62 **(10)-** *...since I have come here from God; yes, I have come from him...I tell you most solemnly, before Abraham ever was, I Am.* Jn. 8:42, 58. **(11)-** *I have come so that they may have life and have it to the full...Yet you say to someone the Father has consecrated and sent into the world...* Jn. 10:10, 36. **(12)-** *...so that they may believe it was you who sent me.* Jn. 11:42. **(13)-** *...and whoever sees me, sees the one who sent me. I, the light, have come into the world...what I had to speak was commanded by the Father, who sent me.* Jn. 12:45-46, 49. **(14)-** *...Jesus knew that the Father had put everything* *into his hands, and that he had come from God and was returning to God…* Jn. 13:3. **(15)-** *Now, Father, it is time for you to glorify me with that glory I had with you before ever the world was…and they have truly accepted this, that I came from you, and have believed that it was you who sent me…As you sent me into the world, I have sent them into the world…because you loved me before the foundation of the world.* Jn. 17:5, 8, 18, 24. **(16)-** *Like an eagle watching its nest, hovering over its young, he spreads out his wings to hold him, he supports him on his pinions.* Deut. 32:11. **(17)-** The Mahabharata contains a story about the gaze pointed to one point alone: *Drona, teacher of military skills, teaches archery to several princess. He sets up a wooden bird upon a tree and consecutively asks his students to aim at the eye of the bird. He asks them what do they see while they set aim at the target. They reply that they see the teacher, the other students, the tree, the river and the bird. Drona does not let them shoot. When testing Arjuna, he replies that he sees only the eye of the bird. Drona asks him to shoot, and Arjuna strikes the bird down in the eye.* Swami Atchyutanand: Yoga of inner light and sound. Publisher: Santmat Satsang Samiti, Chandrapur, India, 2011, page 23.

Stanza 32 (1)- *God is such that if people live in harmony with him and do his will, he will give them whatever they want; but if they seek their own interests it will be useless for them to speak to God.* John, *Works*, Ascent Book 3 Chapter 44 paragraph 3 page 346 **(2)-** See stanza 31 and note 31.2. **(3)-** See note 19.5 **(4)-** *In making these gifts, he has given us the guarantee of something very great and wonderful to come: through them you will be able to share the divine nature…*2 Peter 1:4. **(5)-** *…indeed, from his fullness we have, all of us, received- yes, grace in return for grace.* Jn. 1:16. (6)- See note 2.12

Stanza 33 (1)- *I am dark but beautiful, daughters of Jerusalem; wherefore the King has loved me and brought me to his inner chamber.* Sg.1. 4-5. **(2)-** *Do not consider that I am brown, because the sun hath altered my colour.* Sg 1.5. **(3)-** *Be not without fear for sin forgiven.* Ecclesiasticus (Ecclus, Eclo., Si.) 5:5. **(4)-** See note 32.5 **(5)-** Esther 6:11 **(6)-** *The king has brought me into his rooms;*

you will be our joy and our gladness. Sg. 1.4-5 **(7)-** *Since you have become honorable and glorious in my sight, I have loved you* (which means: after I had turned my eyes toward you, thus giving you grace and making you glorious, you merited the grace of more of my favors) Is. 43:4 **(8)-** *For anyone who has will be given more, and he will have more than enough; but from anyone who has not, even what he has will be taken away.* Lk 19:26; Mt 13:12

Stanza 34 (1)- ...*As the apple-tree among the trees of the woods, so is my beloved among the sons. I sat down under his shadow, whom I desired; and his fruit was sweet to my palate.* Sg. 2.3. **(2)-** *Anyone who exalts himself will be humbled, and anyone who humbles himself will be exalted.* Mt. 23:12; Lk. 14:11. **(3)-** See note 11.1 (Sg 2.14). **(4)-** (The Bride says): *"How beautiful you are, my Beloved, and how delightful!"* Sg 1: 15. **(5)** -*Then he sent out the dove, to see whether the waters were receding from the surface of the earth. The dove, finding nowhere to perch, returned to him in the ark, for there was water over the whole surface of the earth; putting out his hand, he took hold of it and brought it back into the ark with him. After waiting seven more days, again he sent out the dove from the ark. In the evening, the dove came back to him and there it was with a new olive-branch in its beak.* Gen. 8:8-11.**(6)-** For it was you who created my being, knit me together in my mother's womb. Ps 138.13 **(7)-** See note 6.1 (St Augustine).

Stanza 35 (1)- *I shall lead her into solitude and there speak to her heart.* Ho. 2:14. **(2)-** *Truly the sparrow has found a house and the turtledove a nest where she can nurture her young.* Ps. 83:4. **(3)-** See note 20.7 (John, *Works*, poem: Without support yet with support) **(4)-** *Everyone moved by the Spirit of God is a son of God.* Rom. 8:14.

Stanza 36 (1)- *Before the day brakes and the shadows retire, I will go to the mountain of myrrh and to the hill of incense ... I to my Beloved and he turns towards me. Come, my Beloved, let us go forth into the field, let us abide together on* *the grange; let us get up very early and go to the vineyards, let us see if the vineyard flourish, if the flowers be ready to bring forth fruits, if the pomegranates flourish; there I will give you my breasts* (i.e. my love). Sg 4:6 and 7:10-12. **(2)-** *All the rest of his life was in joy, practising almsgiving and continually praising God and extolling his greatness.* Tob. 14:2. **(3)-** *Then your light will rise up in darkness, and your darkness will be as the noonday. And your Lord God will give you rest always and will fill your soul with brightness…withdrawing your paths and ways to quietude…if you glorify him by not doing your own paths and not fulfilling your own will, then you will delight in the Lord…* Is. 58:10-14. **(4)-** Outward exercise of love by means of *Acts*: see Stanza 3… *I will neither gather flowers not fear wild beasts…* **(5)-** See comment to stanza 29… *that, stricken by love, I intentionally lost myself, and was gained.* **(6)-** *…all I have is yours and all you have is mine…* Jn. 17:10. **(7)-** *How rich are the depths of God- how deep his wisdom and knowledge- and how impossible to penetrate his motives or understand his methods!* Rom. 11:33. **(8)-** *Mine are the heavens and mine is the Earth. Mine are the nations, the just are mine, and mine are the sinners. The angels are mine, and the Mother of God, and all things are mine; and God himself is mine and for me, because Christ is mine and all for me. What do you ask, then, and seek, my soul? Yours is all of this, and all is for you. Do not engage yourself in something less or pay heed to the crumbs that fall from your Father's table. Go forth and exult in your Glory! Hide yourself in it and rejoice, and you will obtain the supplications of your heart.* John, *Works*, Sayings of Light and Love, nr. 27. **(9)-** *The precepts of Yahweh are…more desirable than gold, even than the finest gold; his words are sweeter than honey, even than honey that drips from the comb.* Ps. 18:9-11. **(10)-** See note 14.2 (Bangar) **(11)-** Passive purgation is necessary. See John, *Works*, Dark Night Book 1 chapter 14. **(12)-** *Who will grant that my request be fulfilled and that God will give me what I hope for and that he who began may destroy me, and let lose his hand and put an end to me? And that I may have this comfort, that in afflicting me with sorrow he might not spare me?* Job 6:8-10. **(13)-** *A genuine spirit seeks rather the distasteful in God than the delectable, leans more toward suffering than toward consolation, more toward* *going without everything for God than toward possession, and toward dryness and affliction than toward sweet consolation. It knows that that is the significance of following Christ and denying self, that the other method is perhaps a seeking of self in God.* John, *Works,* Ascent, Book II Chapter 7, paragraph 5.

Stanza 37 (1)- *…the blossoming vines give out their fragrance. Arise, make haste, my love, my beautiful one, and come into the clefts of the rock and into the cavern of the wall…There you will teach me, and I shall give you the drink of spiced wine and of juice from my pomegranates.* Sg. 2:13-14 and 8:2. **(2)-** *And when my glory shall pass, I will set thee in a hole of the rock…* Ex. 33:22. **(3)-** *……since they all drank from the spiritual rock that followed them as they went, and that rock was Christ…* 1 Cor. 10:4. **(4)-** *…so that your understanding may come to full development, until you really know God's secret, in which all the jewels of wisdom and knowledge are hidden.* Col. 2:2-3. **(5)-** See notes 14.2 and 36.7

Stanza 38 (1)- *There you will teach me, and I shall give you a drink of spiced wine and of juice from my pomegranates.* Sg. 8.2. **(2)-** *…the love of God has been poured into our hearts by the Holy Spirit, which has been given us.* Rom. 5:5. **(3)-** *Now we are seeing a dim reflection in a mirror; but then we shall be seeing face to face. The knowledge that I have now is imperfect; but then I shall know as fully as I am known.* 1 Cor. 13:12. **(4)-** Sg. 3:11 **(5)-** *…you anticipated him with blessings of sweetness and set on his head a crown of precious stones.* Ps. 20:3. **(6)-** *Yahweh, how great your goodness, reserved for those who fear you, bestowed on those who take shelter on you….* Ps. 30:20. **(7)-** *They drink from the stream of your delight.* Ps. 35:9. **(8)-** *Eye has not seen, outside of you, Lord, what you have prepared…* Is. 64:4. **(9)-** *The things that no eye has seen and no ear has heard, things beyond the mind of man, all that God has prepared for those who love him.* 1 Cor. 2:9. **(10)-** *To him that overcomes I will give to eat the tree of life, which is in the paradise of my God.* Rev. 2:7. **(11)-** *Be faithful unto death and I will give you the crown of life.* Rev. 2:10. **(12)-** *To the one who overcomes I will give the* *hidden manna and a white stone, and on the stone a new name will be written, which no one knows save the one who receives it.* Rev. 2:17. **(13)-** *To the one who overcomes and keeps my commandments until the end I will give power over the nations. That one will rule them with a rod of iron, and as a vessel of clay they shall be smashed, as I also received of my Father. And I will give that one the morning star.* Rev. 2:26-28. **(14)-** *The one who overcomes will thus be clothed in white garments, and I will not cross the name of that one from the book of life. And I will confess this name before my Father.* Rev. 3:5. **(15)-** *And I will make the one who overcomes a pillar in the temple of my God, and this victor shall go out no more. And I will write upon this one the name of my God and the name of the city of my God, and also my new name.* Rev. 3:12. **(16)-** *To the one who overcomes I will give to sit with me on my throne, as I also have conquered and sat with my Father on his throne. Let whoever has ears to hear, hear…* Rev. 3:21-22. **(17)-** See note 34.6

Stanza 39 (1)- *…the voice of the turtledove is heard in our land …the vines in flower have given their fragrance… let your voice sound in my ears, for your voice is sweet…* Sg. 2. 12-14. **(2)-** *The night will be my illumination in my delights.* Ps. 138:11. **(3)-** *Our Lord is a consuming fire.* Deut. 4:24. **(4)-** (Christ speaks): *"(the soul) dies to itself wholly, daughter, in order that it may fix itself more and more upon Me; it is no longer itself that lives, but I. As it cannot comprehend what it understands, it is an understanding which understands not."* One who has experienced this, will understand something of it; it cannot be more clearly expressed, since all that comes to pass in this state is so obscure. Teresa, Works, Life Chapter 18 page 110. **(5)-** *The godliest knowledge of God is that which is known through ignorance.* The cloud of unknowing, anonymous English Carthusian from 13th Century, Penguin Books, 2001, London, chapter 70 page 96 **(6)-** *Who can keep back the Word conceived within and not say it?* Job 4:2. **(7)-** *Since you are children of God, God sent the Spirit of his Son into your hearts, calling to the Father.* Gal. 4:6. **(8)-** *The power to be children of God.* Jn. 1:12. **(9)-** *I pray not only for these, but for those also who through their words will believe in me. May all be one, Father, may they be one in us, as you are in me* *and I am in you, so that the world may believe it was you who sent me. I have given them the glory you gave to me, that they may be one as we are one. With me in them and you in me, may they be so completely one that the world will realize that it was you who sent me and that I have loved them as much as you have loved me. Father, I want those you have given me to be with me where I am, so that they may always see the glory you have given me...* Jn. 17:20-24. **(10)-** *May you have more and more grace and peace as you come to know our Lord more and more. By his divine power, he has given us all the things that we need for life and for true devotion, bringing us to know God himself, who has called us by his own glory and goodness. In making these gifts, he has given us the guarantee of something very great and wonderful to come: through them you will be able to share the divine nature...* 2 Peter 1:2-4. **(11)-** *Arise, make haste, my love, my dove, my beautiful one, and come! For the winter is now passed, the rains are over and gone, and the flowers have appeared in our land, the time of pruning has come, and the voice of the turtledove is heard in our land. The fig tree has put forth her fruits; the vines in flower give their fragrance. Arise, my love, my fair one, and come!* Sg. 2: 10- 14. **(12)-** JS Bach, Christmas Carol, In dulce iubilo **(13)-** *Through Christ, with Him, in Him, to you, Almighty Father, in the unity of the Holy Spirit, all glory and honor is yours, now and forever, amen.* The Order of the Mass, Doxology.

Stanza 40 (1)- Aminadab is the Devil (Sg 6.11) **(2)-** *I went down into the garden of nuts to see the fruits of the valleys, and to look if the vineyard had flourished and the pomegranates budded. I knew not; my soul troubled me for the chariots of Aminadab.* Sg 6.10- 11 (Vulgate Douay, English). St. Jerome had translated from Greek as *Descendi ad hortum nucum ut viderem poma convallis ut inspicerem si floruisset vinea et germinassent mala punica. Nescivi, anima mea conturvabit me, propter quadrigas Aminadab* (Biblia Sacra Vulgatae, Latin). A more recent translation is *I went down to the nut orchard to see what was sprouting in the valley, to see if the vines were budding and the pomegranate trees in flower. Before I knew, my desire had hurled me on the chariots of my people, as their prince* (Jerusalem Bible). (see Introduction, notes 4-6) **(3)-** *Who is* *this that comes up from the desert, flowing with delights, leaning upon her Beloved, diffusing love everywhere?* Sg. 8:5. **(4)-** It is to be noted that in Yoga and Samkya psychology, developed with much greater use of introspection than Western psychology, the imagination and the mind (*chitta, citta*) are considered matter, part of the material world (*prakriti*). Karambelkar PV: Patañjala Yoga Sutras, Kaivalyadhama, Lonavla, India 1987 page 6. **(5)-** *My heart and my flesh have rejoiced in the living God.* Ps. 83:3. **(6)-** *The water that I shall give will turn into a spring inside him, welling up eternal life.* Jn. 4:14.

www.ingramcontent.com/pod-product-compliance
Lightning Source LLC
LaVergne TN
LVHW051600070426
835507LV00021B/2682